SCENE PAINTING
AND DESIGN

SCENE PAINTING AND DESIGN

BY
STEPHEN JOSEPH

WITH A FOREWORD BY
SEAN KENNY

LONDON
SIR ISAAC PITMAN & SONS LTD.

First published 1964
Reprinted 1965

SIR ISAAC PITMAN & SONS Ltd.
PITMAN HOUSE, PARKER STREET, KINGSWAY, LONDON, W.C.2
THE PITMAN PRESS, BATH
PITMAN HOUSE, BOUVERIE STREET, CARLTON, MELBOURNE
22–25 BECKETT'S BUILDINGS, PRESIDENT STREET, JOHANNESBURG

ASSOCIATED COMPANIES
PITMAN MEDICAL PUBLISHING COMPANY Ltd.
46 CHARLOTTE STREET, LONDON, W.I

PITMAN PUBLISHING CORPORATION
20 EAST 46TH STREET, NEW YORK, N.Y. 10017

SIR ISAAC PITMAN & SONS (CANADA) Ltd.
(INCORPORATING THE COMMERCIAL TEXT BOOK COMPANY)
PITMAN HOUSE, 381–383 CHURCH STREET, TORONTO

©

Stephen Joseph

1964

MADE IN GREAT BRITAIN AT THE PITMAN PRESS, BATH
F5—(G.383)

FOREWORD

By SEAN KENNY

WHATEVER we may say about the theatre today—about its excitement, its glamour and greatness, its new waves and new inventions—the sad truth is that it is not a very important happening in the lives of most people. It has little to do with the carrying-on of life. Its voice is generally meek and if not meek then certainly muffled. It is there for the few and, because of the few, is becoming more and more ingrown on itself. Its excitement is perverted and its truths appear to be dull and naïve. Like music, painting, and sculpture it has become a useless hobby, something to indulge in, a false culture worn only to impress. No art form is real unless it speaks from a necessity, out of a genuine feeling for excitement and truth. This feeling must be born of its own time and place, and it uses whatever form of language the artist finds easiest to speak through. Accepting art in worn-out formulae and moulds of dead styles is the dangerous habit pushed upon us by the conditioning process of the *experts*. The idea that the voice used well once is the only voice worth using can only be the sales talk of self-satisfied museum managers.

It is not the fault of the people that what is called *art* does not attract them—it has nothing to do with their lives or the price of their bread or even what they look for outside the normal pattern of living. It is inaccessible and remote, a thing that must always be incomprehensible; something which is owned and paid for by a precious minority.

Forget all *Art and Culture* labels attached to theatre and try to see how we can make this one form of art a live, real, exciting voice! Forget all habits and old-fashioned ways of presenting theatre and begin again to think: how can one best tell a story to a group of people?

Technically the theatre has much ground to make up and vast areas to explore. New ways of presentation can revitalize old and threadbare plays. A fresh approach here is needed now more than ever. We cannot change the design of our theatre

buildings overnight. Therefore while we wait for new places
we must examine and use to their fullest capabilities the theatres
that we have; their insides—the stage and the auditorium.
Much can be done on our existing stages. Too often directors
and designers are satisfied with a few flats set up as the old box
set. It seems that the more limitations that are imposed
economically and spatially on companies the more they try
to build (and improve on) the largest, overdesigned box
settings. The whole idea of design should be to arrange the
stage and add to it only whatever is necessary for a particular
show. Whatever is absolutely necessary should be enough.
In this way—by the selection and design of the visual elements
arising out of the action and the story itself—good stage design
would emerge. A few basic pieces well designed are far better
than an enormous hodge-podge of elaborately moulded flats,
ceilings and complicated structures. How else can stage design
improve, or indeed become a valid part of theatre, if it does
not seek to understand the force of the selective eye? Good
stage design is the effort to place and support the story in a
visually exciting way. Too often designers work straight from
the stage directions in the script and not from the heart of the
story and the idea itself.

The theatre at the moment is full of lazy wishy-washy people
who are too easily satisfied with what is. They take all for
granted. They never ask the question: why is it there at all?
It is people like Mr. Stephen Joseph who give the theatre its
life blood and vitality. They ask questions—even about the
Emperor's new clothes. The energy and excitement we are
looking for will come from them. Mr. Joseph is a devoted
addict of the drama and, as a professional working member of
the theatre, takes a look at the field of design. It is only too
rarely that our real professionals find time to speak on aspects
of their work in the theatre. I don't know how he found the
time but I'm delighted Stephen Joseph stayed with the type-
writer long enough to write this book.

CONTENTS

LIST OF PLATES

(Between pages 44 and 45)

ILLUSTRATIONS IN TEXT

ACKNOWLEDGEMENTS

I HAVE had help from many different people in the prepara-
tion of this book and would like to express my gratitude to
them here. Percy Corry started me on the book, read the
proofs and made useful suggestions. Sean Kenny has given me
encouragement, particularly by contributing an introduction.
Disley Jones offered the set of drawings, facing pages 110 and
111, for *South*, and his own photographs of the design, model and
set (Plates III and IV). I am also grateful to the directors of
theatres, amateur and professional, who sent me photographs
and drawings to choose from, and to photographers for permission to reproduce them: to Lawrence Weigall for Plate I;
Strand Electric, London, for Plate II; Nicholas Horne Ltd.,
Totnes, for Plate V (*upper*); L. du Garde Peach for Plate V
(*lower*); R. B. Grierson, Frinton-on-Sea, for Plate VI (*upper*);
Angus McBean for Plates VI (*lower*) and VII; Arthur Hamer,
Manchester, for Plate VIII; E. A. Meyer, Lewes, for Plate
IX; Roy Brown for Plate X (*upper*); Walkers Studios,
Scarborough, for Plate XI (*lower*); Kenneth Jepson for Plate
XI (*upper*); Commercial Studios, Ipswich, for Plates XI (*lower*)
and XII (*lower*); Edward G. Bent, Hornchurch, for Plate XII
(*upper*); H. N. Davis, Oldham, for Plate XIII; W. Dennett,
Guildford, for Plate XIV (*upper*); Leslie Studios, Rotherham,
for Plates XIV (*lower*) and XVI; Derek Gardner, Leatherhead,
for Plate XV (*upper*); and Hartley L. H. Laurence, Lincoln,
for Plate XV (*lower*). I am indebted to the Strand Electric and
Engineering Company for permission to use the photograph on
Plate II; to Ronald Kay for the drawing on page 85; and to
Stephen Garrett who helped me with the sequence of drawings
on pages 76 and 77.

I

INTRODUCTORY

IN any big theatre the production of a play is likely to be
a complicated business involving many people—actors,
author, producer, director, designer, musicians, manager, stage
director and a host of staff, assistants and tradesmen; yet the
play itself must appear before the audience as a single organic
whole. The person usually responsible for welding together all
the separate contributions of so many different people is the
producer. In the American theatre, and sometimes in ours, he
is called the director. And we may as well admit now that it is
extremely difficult to arrive at an exact terminology when we
are talking about theatre. Names of different people and things
are used in different ways. We shall meet this difficulty again.

To return to the producer—he may do more than supervise
the whole proceedings. He may act in his own production.
Indeed, he may be primarily an actor. He may design his own
scenery. The smaller the theatre and company presenting the
play, the more likely it is that the producer will contribute in
such ways. In a very small company, such as the tiny summer
theatre at Frinton-on-Sea where I worked many years ago, the
producer may be manager, stage director, lighting designer,
scenic artist and actor as well. Certainly all these jobs came
my way!

There is a very real advantage in keeping control over so
many aspects of production; it obviously increases the chances
of stylistic unity. Even in very small companies, however (and
certainly in large ones), the designer usually works independently of the producer. The designing and painting of scenery
constitute a highly specialized and technical subject. It is the
aim of this book to explore some of the elements in that
technique.

The Scene Designer's Duties

The scene designer is generally responsible not only for
scenery itself but also, when the production calls for them,

costumes, masks, furniture, and properties. He will design them, make, borrow or buy them, paint them and arrange them on the stage. He may be called on to arrange the lighting. His realm includes all the visual aspects of production other than those contributed by the actors themselves in movement and personal appearance. Sometimes he will take care of the actors' make-up as well. When there is any doubt about them his exact responsibilities will probably be outlined by the producer. He must be prepared to do a large number of things. This book will cover only a limited amount of ground, and, as far as possible, it will concentrate on scenery: the designer should know how it is made, and why; what materials it is made of, how it is painted, shifted and set up; how it is lit. This much knowledge is essential and an attempt can be made to discuss it in this book.

The designer will also find it useful to know how scenery fits into different sorts and sizes of theatre; what it means to actors and stage staff; what the fire regulations say, and why. His job will be easier if he knows something about acting, music, playwriting and all the other elements of production. Obviously the range is wider than can be covered in a single book.

Qualities and Talents Required in a Designer

What sort of a person should the designer be? You would expect him to have certain natural talents and personal qualities. He should have a vigorous interest in people and their backgrounds, the clothes they wear, the rooms they live in, the cities and countries they inhabit, and the natural landscape behind them, both nowadays and in other times. Such material can be observed in everyday life, in museums, in paintings, photographs, and in magazines and catalogues. From these sources he can make a personal collection of reference material. He should have the ability to translate ideas and emotions into visual images and, particularly since his work is sometimes far from photographic, he should understand formal and spatial relationships and the value of colour. He should be an artist, abreast of modern trends and tendencies as well as aware of the inheritance from the Renaissance. He should know what he owes to those artists who, like Brunelleschi, Raphael and Leonardo, were architects, engineers civil and military, poets, sculptors and painters. They forged cannon, laid sewers and built bridges, and, as well, they decorated walls and ceilings (with countless masterpieces), and they designed costumes and scenery which have vanished as all such ephemeral things do. Even nowadays it is at least worth aiming at achieving their sort of versatility. The separation of the artist from the practical man, the man of science, is a lifeless division. In the building of scenery it can lead to disaster, as when, for instance, the beautiful design turned into scenery fails to stand up on the stage! That catastrophe, at least, can be avoided.

You might say that the designer should direct his talent in four different ways. Firstly, he should cultivate those particular skills that belong to him purely as a designer. Secondly, he should develop an unrestricted interest in every form of human activity in order to have a good supply of source material. Thirdly, he should have a good working knowledge of related skills in the theatre, and in the other arts and sciences. Finally, he should encourage his own original and creative ideas and strive to contribute to the living, growing, exciting and unpredictable phenomenon called theatre. It is a tall order. This book can only be expected to nudge the designer's elbow gently, and give him some basic information. I hope the facts are accurate even where the information is incomplete. And if some of the material seems irrelevant I hope no one will dismiss it too quickly. The danger of having a tidy mind is that there may not be much room for good ideas to grow. I have not tried to write a complete handbook of instructions, though I have given plenty of instructions, but I have rambled here and there hoping that I may provide a stimulus. It is my own habit to skip from one subject to another. If I have been able to impose order on the material in this book it is mainly due to the training I received from Professor Arnold Gillette. I studied scene design under him for a year at the State University of Iowa. It was a discipline I needed, and for which I am very grateful.

II

WHAT IS SCENERY?

MOST people who know anything at all about the theatre would tell you at once that scenery consists of flats and cloths. They serve two functions on the stage. They provide a background for the actors, and they screen the walls, spaces and machinery backstage from the audience's view. Let us examine each of these functions independently.

Flats and Cloths as Background

Many modern plays are set in a room. On the stage the setting may consist of five more or less plane surfaces—three walls (the fourth being open for the audience's benefit, of course), a floor and a ceiling. Many small companies ignore the floor and ceiling, but a good designer will always take them into consideration. The design may call for only two walls when the room is viewed from an angle. But the principle is the same. The ceiling may cover only part of the setting, or it may be entirely open except for borders. But where there is a scenic ceiling it is made in the same way as the walls—of flats.

A flat is a rectangular framework of wood covered with canvas. A set of flats, which will usually all be of the same height though of different widths, and include some constructed to take doors, windows or fireplaces, can be arranged in many different ways. This versatility is useful simply because so many plays are set in rooms. The structure of flats arranged to represent a room is usually called a box set. Through the windows of a box set a view painted on a cloth is likely to be seen. A cloth is a rectangular expanse of canvas hanging from a horizontal batten and weighted down at the bottom by another batten. A groundrow supplies the suggestion of middle distance, and it is usually made of a flat that is long in proportion to its height (it is often a standard flat set on its side) and it may have an irregular profile.

All this scenery offers the designer flat surfaces that can be treated much in the way that a painter treats his canvas. Once the flats have been arranged to suggest the shape of the room, the designer's job may appear to be that of an interior decorator, and many small companies accept this. I have seen sets where the walls have been painted just as a room might be decorated; I have even seen wallpaper put on to flats. The result is nearly always distressing. The audience is not in the position of someone in such a room, and lighting on stage is quite different from the lighting in a room. Mere interior decoration simply will not work on stage to give the appearance of a room; light and distance must be reckoned with. Further, age and texture will have to be conveyed in paint, as well as any imaginative toning related to the atmosphere and intention of the play. More of this later on.

Flats and Cloths to Mask in the Acting Area

The second function of flats and cloths is to mask in the acting area. The space and machinery used for shifting and storing scenery must be hidden from the view of the audience. Backstage walls must be entirely concealed—except for deliberate and special effect. A famous production of *Our Town* left the entire backstage open, but this was a special requirement, designed to emphasize the theatricality of the production, in which, incidentally, the stage manager played a part. In *Oliver* at the New Theatre, in London, Sean Kenny made careful and deliberate use of the back wall on which he painted the background. It was a background of London's houses and the brickwork of the wall gave a magnificently appropriate texture to the scene. But where a box set is used, a convention is established, and to see through the setting is to destroy its validity.

Both these functions (masking and providing a background) apply to other forms of setting that make use of flats. Where flats are used to make up sets of wings, with borders and backcloth, they still form a background to the acting and conceal the room backstage. You might suppose that backstage could be concealed by lighting only the acting area, but this would make it difficult to work backstage. The idea is valid, however, for forms of open stage which we shall discuss shortly, and it is a reminder that light behind the scenes must be kept within limits so as not to intrude on the acting area nor be seen by the audience.

Three-dimensional Scenery

In addition to flats and cloths already mentioned, the box set nearly always uses some three-dimensional scenery. There are usually such pieces as doors, windows, fireplaces or stairs. Many theatres keep not only a stock of flats and cloths, but also a quantity of these three-dimensional pieces to go with them, and, in addition, a number of rostrum units to make platforms of different levels. Further, scenery includes three-dimensional pieces of irregular shape and such natural objects as trees, rocks and hillocks besides all sorts of abstract shapes on the ground and in the air. Because of the immense variety of three-dimensional pieces the design problems they present are usually functional and structural. They can be made of all sorts of materials. The scope for an imaginative designer is unlimited.

Now, the moment you begin to explore the possibilities of three-dimensional scenery, you will see that it can be used quite independently of flats. For example, many exciting designs by Norman Bel Geddes or by Terence Gray are made up entirely of architectural shapes. Flats define the acting area like a boundary, solid units provide a centre to the acting area. Flats are peripheral, solid units are focal. It is as though flats were part of a technique of presentation depending on the conventions of painting, while solid scenery depends on the conventions of sculpture. This idea is fairly obvious for a start, but it leads on to other interesting ones that are perhaps not quite so obvious. For instance a painting is usually framed, and the proscenium arch or picture frame is part of the convention of the enclosed stage in the theatre as we know it. The frame derives from the Renaissance in Italy; its function was to circumscribe the area of illusion—the illusion of the third dimension. Sculpture does not require a frame, it is verifiably in three dimensions. Need we have a frame round three-dimensional scenery? If not, why set it on an enclosed stage? Then again, you look at a picture, for the most part, from fair and square in front of it. In just the same way it is the centre seats of the theatre that are best. But most sculpture can be, and indeed should be looked at from all round. Is it possible that solid scenery might benefit from an audience surrounding the acting area? In other words, the use of solid

scenery begins to suggest the open stage. Equally, if you have
an open stage it may be as well to start off with the intention
of using solid scenery.

The Development of the Stage

It is true that most people who work in theatre are used to an
enclosed stage. Nearly all our theatres have an enclosed stage,
and halls, when they are adapted for theatrical purposes,
usually aim at imitating this established form. But the Mermaid
Theatre in London, the Festival Theatre at Chichester and the
Victoria Theatre at Stoke-on-Trent, and many theatres abroad,
have open stages. Adaptations of existing halls, for professional
and amateur drama, are increasingly allowing for the open stage;
it nearly always offers a more satisfactory way of adapting an
ordinary hall than the enclosed stage. So let us leave the subject
of scenery for a moment to take a closer look at the theatre itself
and see what the open stage really is, and why the enclosed stage
has come to dominate our theatre during recent times.

We know very little about the staging techniques of ancient
drama. The reason for this is obvious; drama precedes
history, it precedes literature, writing and, probably, language
itself. It is the first art of civilized mankind. It begins as dance,
there is no scenery, only the background of spectators who
surround the performers and, beyond them, the natural landscape. There may be a campfire in the centre of the arena and
flames to illuminate the dancers after nightfall, casting shadows
towards the watchers, and smoke ascending to the dark ceiling
of the sky punctured by stars and the moon. Men dance to
assert themselves, to catch the attention of the gods or other
magical powers, to gain their will over the indifferent universe.
To increase their power they use costumes and masks and
disguise—the first purely technical requirement of the actor.
The progress of drama is marked, in time, by the introduction
of words which are the beginnings of song and poetry and soon
evolve into literature as we know it. Then comes the arrangement of the place, the meeting place of the actors and their
audience. This is the beginning of theatre as a structure.

The reason for a special structure is simple. When many
people stand round and watch, those at the back cannot see the
performers over the heads of the people in front of them.

There are two ways of dealing with the situation. The actors can be raised, on a cart, perhaps, as Thespis is supposed to have been, or the audience can be raised row by row as the Greeks were on their hillsides, or both actors and audience can be raised. The precise method used has characterized the forms of theatre that took shape during the centuries in which drama has flourished.

The Cart and the Auditorium

The cart, perhaps the most primitive stage structure, has sometimes been replaced by boards and trestles and sometimes by a more solid platform, and survives still in the modern theatre as a truck stage. Essentially the cart is mobile, limited in size, and invites decoration. It became, in the hands of medieval tradesmen, the pageant cart got up entire to represent a particular place—Heaven or Hell-mouth, the house of Pilate or the Ark of Noah. A series of such carts could set forth a moving picture of the whole Bible story—Apocrypha included —from the creation of the world to the last day of judgement. Artists of the Renaissance elaborated on the pageant cart for magnificent displays of welcome and rejoicing in terms allegorical, symbolical or just plain flamboyant. A good impression of the results can be got from Denis van Alsloot's paintings of "Isabella's Triumph" in the Victoria and Albert Museum. In a more modest way, a decorated cart could be brought into a hall during a disguising or other court entertainment, as it can still be brought on to any stage as a boat truck. In every example, except perhaps the last, the cart is three dimensional, sculptural and should be viewed from every angle.

The cart may have suggested the most simple of all specially built stages, the booth stage. The booth stage is no more than some planks laid on trestles (or barrels or boxes, perhaps) with a curtained enclosure at one end built with the help of some poles and rope. In one form or another the booth stage is almost universal. It is the simplest device by which an actor can put himself in a position to command the attention of a fairly large audience. It can be swiftly taken to pieces and swiftly erected. It can be carried easily with the help of a pack animal in places (and in other times) where the going is too hard for a cart, and, like the cart, it is capable of all sorts of developments.

The cart is a stage or part of a stage. When, however, to achieve good sight lines, the rows of spectators are raised, a different situation arises. The acting area can remain at ground level as an arena rather than a stage. And while the stage implies a limitation to the acting area, raising the spectators implies a limitation to the auditorium. A stage can be mobile and the audience may move round it. A raised auditorium is

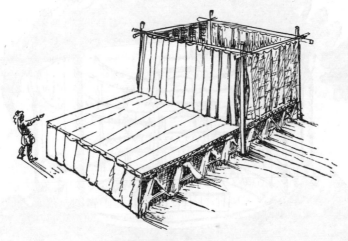

FIG. 1. A BOOTH STAGE

static simply because it is too large a structure to move—though some modern theatres have a revolving auditorium, but even then the relationship of the seats to each other is static. Further, at its simplest, in ancient Greece, when the hillside provided the slope for the audience, a limitation arises from the fact that hillsides are not usually circular (except perhaps the occasional crater) and in Greece at any rate, during its final phase of development, the dancing floor was only partially surrounded by the audience. Such an arrangement immediately suggests a formalized shell. The Romans took the development further and built theatres without relying on the hillsides. Their architectural skill enabled them to return also to the basic theatre form for their large-scale entertainments in such buildings as the Colosseum where the arena is entirely surrounded by seating rows. These shells, whether the acting area is wholly or only partially surrounded by the

audience, do not invite scenic decoration at all. Any decoration
would be essentially architectural. Obviously a cart can be
brought into the arena, as it was at a later date into the bear-
baiting pits and inn-yards of Tudor England. Once there the

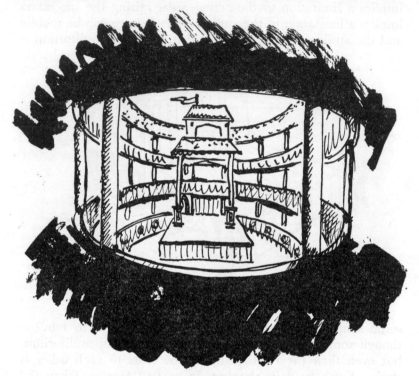

FIG. 2. AN ELIZABETHAN STAGE
(After the famous Swan drawing by de Witt)

cart tends to attach itself to the shell and become part of the
architecture. It then loses its scenic trappings and provides a
more substantial and permanent background for performance.
This seems to have been what happened with such theatres as
the famous Globe of Shakespeare's day. The scenic cart lost
its characteristics and became part of the architectural shell.

The only remaining development in the theatre comes when
it has moved indoors and lighting by artificial means is necessary. Indeed, electricity represents the most important modern
contribution to drama.

FIG. 3. AN OPEN STAGE

An impression of the stage at the Chichester Festival Theatre

The Open Stage

At present there are three forms of open stage in use, and each may be described by the relationship between the acting area and the auditorium. The first, the end stage is a platform set across one end of a fairly long rectangular hall. The second, the three-sided stage can best be described as a rectangular platform with three sides open to the audience, while the fourth

FIG. 4. A THEATRE IN THE ROUND
The temporary arrangement at the Library Theatre in Scarborough

side is a scenic wall. In fact the stage need not be rectangular. It is sometimes circular, trapezoid, polygonal or some other shape, but the lines of sight of the audience, in plan, swing through three-quarters of a circle. The third, the central stage, is completely surrounded by the audience. Since this form of theatre usually makes use of an arena rather than a raised platform it is more often called theatre in the round, though, again, the acting area may be any shape as long as the audience is all round it. There are many other possible forms of open stage. A particularly interesting one is a hybrid between the enclosed stage and the open stage, championed by many directors including Peter Hall who would like something of the sort at Stratford-on-Avon for the presentation of Shakespeare's plays. A fully flexible open-stage theatre is another interesting idea that reflects the work of Okhlopkov in the twenties at the Realist Theatre in Moscow. An interesting plan for an auditorium in a quarter circle, with rows of seats sweeping round to focus on a corner stage, was devised by Norman Bel Geddes in 1933 for the Chicago World Fair. Something related in plan has been adopted by James Hull Miller for the community theatre at Western Springs, Illinois. Other variants include reconstructions of historical forms such as the medieval theatre in the round with its peripheral stages, described by Richard Southern; the transverse stage, described by Leslie Hotson, and the Shakespearian stage as described by such writers as Walter Hodges and Cranford Adams. Each of these may have a particular application in modern times.

The Enclosed Stage

The history of the enclosed stage has so far not been considered in this account. This is fair enough if only because the enclosed stage can be treated quite by itself. Indeed, most books on the theatre deal only with the proscenium theatre, which is, after all, the commonest sort of theatre in England and is likely to remain so for many years to come. To concentrate on open stages for a moment may be a stimulating change, but a book on scenic design must inevitably be concerned primarily with the enclosed stage which, after all, makes most use of scenery. So we must now say something about it.

The proscenium theatre, as I have already hinted, derives from two activities of the Renaissance in Italy. The first was the interest in ancient Greece and Rome. A book on architecture by the Roman author Vitruvius gave the Italians ideas for the design of theatres, and for methods of changing scenes by such devices as *periaktoi*. Vitruvius was accepted as an authority, but what the Italians supposed to be classical concepts were often without any precedent. They had their own obsessions. Their artists, who passed so easily from sculpture and reliefs to surface painting, became fascinated by the whole question of perspective. They examined it scientifically, and used their discoveries to gain mastery of the three-dimensional appearance conveyed on the two-dimensional surface of flat painting and the restricted three-dimensional

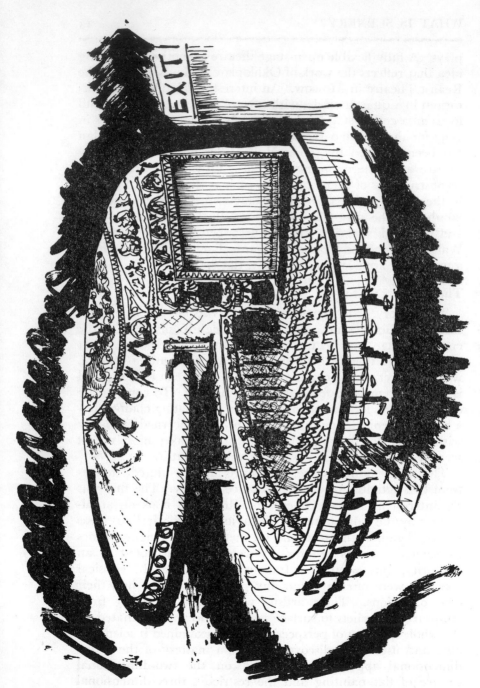

EXIT

FIG. 5. THE AUDITORIUM OF A CONVENTIONAL PROSCENIUM THEATRE

volume of relief. In a painting of the Italian Renaissance the area of the vertical plane of illusion was framed. Within this area, as it were, the miracle of depth was achieved. The superb colour and the convincing perspective were the result as much of scientific study as creative genius. Artists were engineers, anatomists and mathematicians. In the pursuit of perspective they studied trigonometry and optics. They used glass and mirrors and the camera obscura. This last was particularly useful. By optical law it projected a scene from nature on to a flat surface. The artist could thus study and abstract the rules of optical perspective. He could imitate the perspective and the colour of the camera obscura when he came to paint a flat surface. But there was one thing he could not transfer to his picture. This was movement. The wish to put movement into a picture was the second impetus to the Renaissance theatre. And the sort of movement they were concerned with was not just the movement of people but also of the sun, the moon, the stars and the clouds, of the sea, rivers and fountains and, quite unobserved in the camera obscura, angels and gods and all the marvellously mobile host of heaven. Their final solution in the theatre depended, of course, on their engineering knowledge, their experience with triumphal pageant cars, combined with what they had read in Vitruvius about classical scenery. A moving picture could be devised by knocking a hole, within the frame that marked the area of illusion, into the next room. There, the picture was painted in a series of flats designed to be moved. You can see immediately where the proscenium arch came from, and why the stage had to be enclosed. In the next room the separate flats were moved by means of ropes and pulleys, winches, levers and grooves. A vast number of fascinating effects could be achieved. While the spectator watched from one room, in the other the painted pieces were moved, and, of course, the machinery and the men who worked it were concealed. That was part of the magic. The enclosed stage began as an independent and spectacular show of pictorial movement, performed in full view of the audience.

During the sixteenth and seventeenth centuries the Italian fashion for moving-picture shows, like so many other Italian fashions, spread through the courts of Europe. It developed in a number of ways, and inspired again by a misunderstanding of the Greek classical drama, singers were put on a platform in front of the picture frame, or music and dancing eked out the entertainment. From such beginnings grew opera and ballet, in the European tradition that we know. With a platform set up in front of the enclosed stage, it became possible to act plays. The conflict of interest between acting and moving scenery gave rise to a convention of dividing the play into scenes with changes of picture alternating with the acts. In due course the acting area was pushed back into the second room. For a brief period at the end of the nineteenth century a glorious combination of acting and moving pictures satisfied large audiences. It was the era of spectacular melodrama. During this period most of the theatres in England were built. By this time the actors were confined almost entirely behind the picture frame. When the invention of emulsion film made projected moving pictures possible, the audience for them was ready-made. But in the theatre it became fashionable to make any changes of scenery behind curtains while the audience, as many as could afford it, left the auditorium for a ritual refreshment.

It may be worth remarking that not only our theatre but all our visual arts are dominated by concepts deriving from the Italian Renaissance. The National Gallery hardly ventures outside this tradition. It might be fruitless to search for a ready-made tradition that could replace what we have inherited from the Renaissance. But I believe that we should be richer if we found out more about other traditions and respected them all, particularly, as far as theatre is concerned, the traditions of primitive and medieval times and of the eastern world which is only just beginning to be swamped by our western traditions. Modern artists such as Braque and Epstein and Pasmore and Klee, to name the first ones that come to mind in a rush of many more, seem to be well aware of the wide range of other traditions. But the theatre in this country is stagnant. It is not just a matter of insularity and conservatism. There is a real relevance in Renaissance values that appeals to us. For all its glories, there is in Renaissance painting, and its godchild the moving-picture theatre, a simple triumph over superficial reality that we can appreciate. The control of colour, perspective, and movement helped the great artists to depict the true appearance of things. It did not prevent them, of course, from exploring the depths and inner meanings of reality. But the surface truth is enough to trap the gullible and pretentious—artist and public alike. I suspect most of us are trapped. Our theatre reflects our materialistic and superficial values.

In recent years the moving picture has found its apotheosis in television. The theatre that was designed for the first moving pictures proved apt for the movies and may now be considered obsolete. It survives as a place to put actors in simply because we have no idea what to replace it with. The auditorium of the primitive open stage is a different thing altogether and is certainly more suitable for the performance of actors than the display of moving pictures. Something essentially theatrical is lost when actors retreat behind the picture frame, and the camera deals with the new situation more effectively. This is why audiences prefer to watch the vertical screen rather than the horizontal acting area of the enclosed stage. It is no coincidence that the scene designer can move easily from the enclosed stage to the film or television studio. Scenic conventions of picture making are much the same in each case. This should comfort the designer if not the actor!

However, at present there are many theatres with enclosed stages, and we can easily summarize their general characteristics. The enclosed stage belongs to a theatre that is essentially built in two rooms. Its most notable feature is the proscenium arch, built into the wall that separates the auditorium from the stage. The auditorium requires pleasing decoration, comfortable seating, and an orientation towards the proscenium arch. The stage house is more or less a machine shop for manipulating, changing and storing scenery. Its common devices are the grid system, revolving stage, truck stages, or elevators. Such machinery needs backstage and wing space as well as overhead space for the grid. These spaces, and the grid in particular, give to the great theatres of Europe their characteristic shape, with a large cubic volume for the stage house. Such theatres are well adapted to staging a repertoire of plays, or of opera and ballet, where each production requires an entirely different set of flats and cloths. Since such theatres are fairly common, touring companies can take their scenery into many different theatres without difficulty. The repertory and touring systems in theatres with an enclosed stage depend on a degree of standardization, and the acceptance of certain minimal requirements. This is often not understood, particularly by civic authorities in this and other countries who come to the business of building theatres with only an ill-digested vision of the picture frame. Actors and designers suffer from the resulting inadequacies.

Many small halls that serve as theatres have the appearance, from the auditorium, of being built as two rooms. In fact, although the stage is enclosed it is in no useful way separate from the auditorium. There is no room for the scenic activities that make the enclosed stage desirable in the first place. The raised stage reduces height where height is most required. Even where a separate stage house has been built, it is often emasculated to satisfy the demands of economy. For example, among theatres built in England during this century for the use of professional companies, the stage tower of the Belgrade theatre in Coventry is not high enough to allow full size cloths to be flown out; the Royalty Theatre in London was designed to take lighting equipment installed on principles derived from arbitrary, inadequate and antiquated installations in unsuitable village halls; the Prince Charles Theatre has entirely inadequate wing space and no overhead flying space whatever. These last two theatres, however, make adequate cinemas, and the Prince Charles, in common with any small hall, will provide a home for a small revue or recital but it hardly qualifies as a theatre. For one reason or another most of our new theatres and halls are technically inadequate. During the last fifty years about five hundred theatres, equipped for full-scale professional presentations, have closed or been pulled down. Since the war only half a dozen new theatres have been built to replace them. Thousands of inadequate halls have been built with enclosed stages that have unsatisfactory backstage facilities, poor sightlines and inefficient stage lighting. In some of these inadequate halls, actors have been driven to try the open stage in desperation. The simple forms of theatre with open stages are nowhere properly housed, except for the isolated examples of the Chichester Festival Theatre and the Mermaid Theatre in London. From the designer's point of view, makeshift theatres cannot offer full scope for scenic display. Instead much of the designer's time and talent must be squandered in order to try to conceal, as far as possible, the shortcomings of the stage from the audience.

The designer and everyone else connected with the theatre can only regret that enclosed and open stages alike are skimped and badly designed, or housed in unsuitable buildings intended for other purposes. The drama must indeed be powerful if it can survive such bad treatment! But, to return to our subject, most theatres, adequate or not, have enclosed stages and require scenery. There are few open stages, and the special use of scenery on such stages does not at present warrant detailed exposition. Conventions of visual presentation change slowly.

Development of Scenery in the Theatre

In its beginnings, theatre is essentially conventional. The dancers are dancers, the setting is the glade or whatever it really is, and if it is decorated it is for decoration's sake. The only technical device used by the actors is disguise. It may be costume, mask or painting on the body. It is decorative, it separates the actors from the audience, it is magical, ritual, sexual and essential. When scenery is first introduced it is as decoration, or as a symbol to replace the real thing—a stick for a horse, a flag for the sea—but it can stand side by side with real things without causing any embarrassment. This is theatre that is ostensibly theatre. It is commenting on reality.

The first theatre of illusion is the Renaissance theatre, and as already noted, it starts with pictures pure and simple. From sculpture, through relief to flat painting, the Renaissance artists tried to capture the appearance of absolute reality, and their theatre was a device, partly architectural and partly pictorial, to extend the illusion of reality into movement. The first settings were made in three dimensions, with solid carving and architectural detail in perspective of the sort you can see in a good relief by Ghiberti or della Robbia or Donatello. There are good examples, originals or casts, in the Victoria and Albert Museum. But scenery as solid as this was heavy, cumbersome and not easy to move, and required more pains to make than its use justified. Painted perspective flats were

the answer. They persisted into the eighteenth century. And
if the settings at Drottningholme or Gripsholme or Schwetz-
ingen look quaint to us and appear to be conventional, they
were intended to provide as absolute an illusion of reality as
was possible at the time. In the early nineteenth century,
realism and illusion received a new impetus from the authentic
staging of Shakespeare's plays, for which archeologists and
scholars did the research work to ensure that the scenery behind
King Lear, Leontes or Hamlet should give an accurate por-
trayal of their historical surroundings—even when the so-called
history was absolute myth. By the end of the nineteenth
century, not only had real rabbits invaded the scenery of *A
Midsummer Night's Dream*, but real horses took the stage for
The Whip. The Victorian spectacular melodrama was a cele-
bration of man's control over the elements. Everything that
appears in nature man can make—or, thought the great
Victorian scientists, soon will be able to—and this would lead
to a paradise on earth. Something to celebrate! Certainly, no
natural scene, however magnificent, defied the painter's art—
and no natural phenomenon, be it thunder, lightning and rain,
snow storm, flood, tempest or typhoon was beyond the means
of the stage. Ships blew up and sank, avalanches buried trains
and the streets of London caught fire. But convention arises
out of established techniques of portraying reality once they
are firmly established. And Strindberg, writing the preface to
Miss Julie in 1888, complained "Nothing is harder than to get
a room that looks something like a room, however easy it may
be for the painter to produce flaming volcanoes and waterfalls.
No doubt the walls must be of canvas, but it really seems time
to draw the line at painting shelves and kitchen utensils on the
canvas. There is so much else that is conventional that we
might be spared the strain involved in believing in painted
saucepans." The demands of Strindberg and Chekhov and
Ibsen for reality on a domestic level were met by new directors
—Stanislavsky, Antoine, and Brahm, whose efforts led to the
establishment of the box set. In the thirties in our own theatre
this became a convention itself—the several doors, the staircase, the high walls, the bookcases, the french windows looking
out on to a garden forever in summer and, with so much
architectural nonsense, the furniture arranged as no one ever

arranged furniture in a room, giving a picture that no longer suggested any sort of reality whatever. It became a sort of wish-fulfilment. A modified version of the box set is still common-place in our own day and age.

The conventional approach to scenery at the end of the nineteenth century led to a number of different styles. The highly formalized shapes of Appia and Craig depended for their effect on the full use of electric lighting—a new tool. Terence Gray's Festival Theatre at Cambridge between the First and Second World Wars explored the possibilities of formal shapes and good lighting; his was, incidentally, almost alone among British theatres in exploring any new scenic style during this time. Constructivism, in the hands of Tairov and Meyerhold, meant a skeleton set, the members of which were usable by actors who interpreted their parts up ladders and poles, on scaffolding and down ropes. The ballet liked things prettier and backcloths were painted by artists unconcerned with photographic reality. For example Picasso designed *The Three-cornered Hat*, Léger did *La Création du Monde*, Chagall, Braque, Dufy, and Marie Laurencin designed for the big canvas on stage. But for the most part the exciting new move-ments of the twenties in Europe passed us by and went to America—and it is from there that we are slowly getting the news of what ground the theatre has covered during the last fifty years. In the U.S.A. a movement towards a tasteful or significant simplicity resulted in magnificent settings by the American designer Robert Edmond Jones. Norman Bel Geddes designed huge architectural abstractions for *Hamlet* and *Lazarus Laughed*, but he will probably be remembered best for his designs for Reinhardt's production of *The Miracle*; he converted a theatre into what appeared to be the interior of a cathedral—and his costume designs were superb. Recently, most American and British design has hovered fairly near the extreme of realism, with only an occasional foray into con-ventionalism. An occasional revue, such as *Share My Lettuce* may be designed with contemporary abstract art as its inspira-tion. Our most talented young designers, such as Sean Kenny and John Bury have a particular penchant for using new materials. They give us a relatively realistic interpretation of background. This seems to be the requirement of today.

3—(G.383)

III

GET TO KNOW YOUR THEATRE

BEFORE starting work on scenery a designer must first know something about the theatre he is to use. The data required can be listed quite simply provided the theatre is, as it probably will be, of the familiar sort with an enclosed stage. If it happens to have an open stage of one kind or another common sense will indicate which of the data are still needed and what other factors should be taken into consideration. Whether he is working with an open or enclosed stage the designer is trying to establish the physical potentialities of the theatre as far as scenery is concerned and to ascertain the sightlines from the auditorium. There are, of course, a number of measurements to be taken. The data can be collected in the order given in the following paragraphs.

Essential Measurements

1. Measure the proscenium opening; measure its width along the proscenium line (that is, the line across the stage immediately behind the proscenium wall). Half this distance, which is often marked on the stage by a brass stud, is the point where, at right-angles to the proscenium line, the centre line will run. Measure the height of the proscenium opening. If there is a permanent border, the height of this above the stage is the distance to be noted. Measure the actual thickness of the proscenium arch and note any oddities in its profile.

2. If the stage juts forward beyond the proscenium line to form a forestage, or apron stage, which may be either permanent or removable, measure its depth along the centre line, its width, its level in relation to stage level and any peculiarities of shape or curvature. Note access from in front of the proscenium by doorways or steps from below, etc., leading backstage. Also note steps leading into the auditorium. Note if there is an orchestra pit. Note provision for footlights and whether or not any footlight trough can be covered over.

3. Note if there is a safety curtain. It usually runs in steel

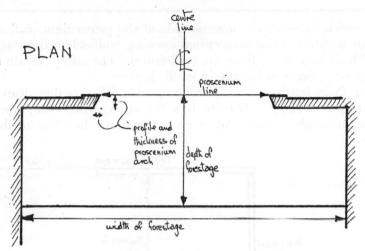

PLAN

centre line

℄

proscenium line

profile and thickness of proscenium arch

depth of forestage

width of forestage

FIG. 6. FORESTAGE PLAN

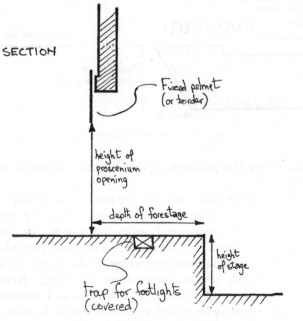

SECTION

Fixed pelmet (or border)

height of proscenium opening

depth of forestage

trap for footlights (covered)

height of stage

FIG. 7. FORESTAGE SECTION

channels fixed on the upstage side of the proscenium wall so that it can seal the proscenium opening and isolate the stage with all its scenery, from the auditorium. The safety curtain is not a requirement in certain small theatres.

4. Note how the main curtains operate, whether they drape, draw, fly or roll. Measure how far upstage they run, from the proscenium line. All stage setting must be clear of the

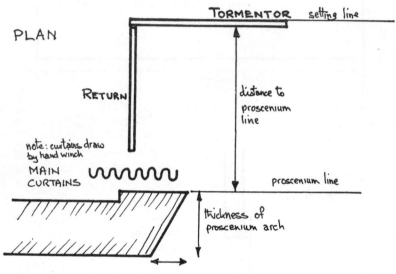

FIG. 8. TORMENTOR/RETURN PLAN

curtain, unless the production deliberately abandons use of the curtain.

5. Mark the position of any permanent or semi-permanent tormentors, teasers and returns. These terms are not always used in the same way and, allowing for elastic meanings, explanation is necessary. Tormentors are flats set roughly parallel to the proscenium line to project on to the stage, thus cutting down the width of the proscenium opening. Returns are flats set at right-angles to the Tormentors and downstage and offstage of them. The teaser is a border which, with the flats just described, helps to form an inner or false proscenium arch. These flats are often faced with black velvet or heavy black twill. They may contain doors or entrances, openings for

perch spots and, almost certainly, a prompter's window. These characteristics should be noted.

6. The grid iron, or grid as it is usually called, is a system of joists forming a ceiling over the stage. It carries blocks arranged so that sets of lines can be rigged for handling scenery. Each set of lines runs parallel to the proscenium line. There are usually three lines to a set and, on stage, these can be attached to the ends and centre of the batten that carries a cloth or other scenery, or a lighting bar. The lines pass over the blocks on the grid and come down to one side of the stage where they can be tied off on cleats which may be fixed in a fly gallery. The grid system allows scenery and equipment to be lowered on to the stage when required, or to be flown out above the stage for storage. It also facilitates a number of more or less complicated flying schemes that may be used in the action of a play, for example in *Peter Pan* where the children fly, and it has given rise to certain spectacular scenic effects, among which the pantomime transformation scene still survives. The grid should be high enough to permit scenery stored over the stage to be right out of sight from the auditorium. This means it should be at least twice as high as any scenery used. Two and a half times the height of the proscenium opening is the formula that is generally accepted for architects to work to. They seldom do. Thus the grid system, which is potentially one of the best and simplest ways of dealing with scenery, is reduced to an expensive and fairly useless convention. But even a conventional gesture in the direction of a grid may provide for supporting lines to carry lighting equipment, etc. At the other extreme, in a good modern theatre lines are counter-weighted and may perhaps be worked by electric winches which are themselves controlled from an electronic console. The designer should note the number of sets of lines, the distance between sets (which is not always constant), which sets of lines are occupied by permanent or semi-permanent equipment, facilities for spot-lines, the safe working load of a set of lines, the system of working, the distance between the centre line and the fly rail (which will mark the maximum width of a cloth), and the overall height of the grid.

7. A theatre may be equipped with a cyclorama or permanent sky-cloth. Its height, width, curvature and colour

should be noted, also its condition, and the possibility of painting on it. When the stage has only a bare brick back wall this should be examined. It may serve as a paintable surface. Note the position of irregular shapes formed by doorways, radiators, fire-fighting apparatus and so on, which should not be on the back wall at all but usually are. The distance from the proscenium line to the sky-cloth, cyclorama or back wall should be measured and noted. The designer should also note whether there is access from one side of the stage to the other without crossing the line between cyclorama (or back wall) and proscenium line. If the actors have access to only one side of the stage, the designer can use the full depth of the stage only with obvious limitations.

8. The stage floor may be raked. That is, it may have a slight slope upwards from the proscenium line to the back wall. The original purpose of this slope was to help the illusion of distance in the perspective pictures of the Renaissance. It has persisted, and now serves no useful purpose other than pleasing certain old-fashioned artists and worshippers of outworn conventions. It is nearly always a nuisance to the designer, to the stage staff and to the actors. It is sometimes wrongly claimed that a raked stage helps sightlines. To have any noticeable effect on sightlines the slope would have to be considerable. A scene designer will sometimes use a steeply sloped platform as part of his setting, but a whole stage cannot be so steeply sloped and remain workable. When, as often happens, the provision of a slightly raked stage is made the excuse for a flat auditorium floor with inadequate sightlines, one can only lament the blinding effect of tradition upon the gullible. However, note the extent of the rake, if any. Note the material and condition of the floor. It should be made of timber that will stand up to the use of stage screws but in school halls, for instance, it is often made of polished hardwood that would be ruined by screws. A stagecloth may be provided and, perhaps, a carpet cut may be fitted for securing its downstage edge.

9. Wing space should be measured on either side of the centre line. Vertical clearance should be checked in the wing spaces, particularly where there is a fly gallery, lighting bridge or other overhead platform.

10. A well-equipped stage may have a revolve or truck stages. These, and other useful devices such as traps, elevators and so on should be measured and located in relation to the proscenium and centre lines.

11. Dock doors, or elephant doors, may be provided so that scenery can easily be brought on to the stage directly from outside or from the workshops. Whatever access to the stage there is should be noted and measured, together with such obstacles and peculiarities as stairways, handrails, doors, windows, radiators and water-cisterns, any of which may be placed so as to frustrate the legitimate movements of a scene

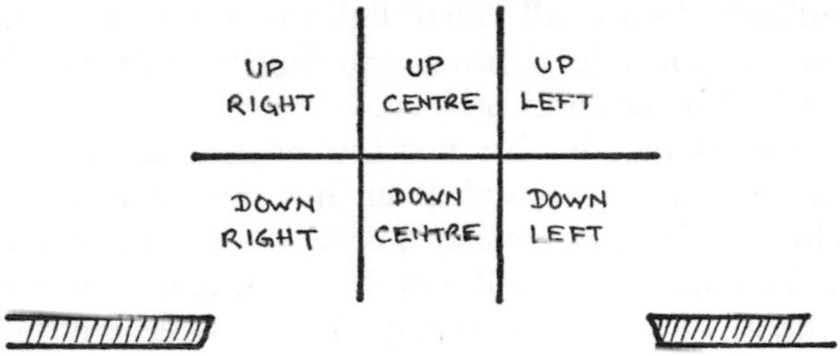

FIG. 9. STAGE DIRECTIONS

designer. They have, of course, their own functions and may suddenly become useful to the designer.

With the information so far assembled, the designer can now make a plan that contains all the measurements on the stage likely to affect a setting, together with an indication of the available methods of putting up and changing sets.

There is a further group of measurements, in the auditorium, that determine the sightlines and that are, therefore, of great importance. When those measurements have been taken it is possible to make plans and sections that will show exactly how much of the stage and of the setting can be seen by everyone in the auditorium. It is usually expected that the audience should see the set and none of the backstage areas.

12. Measure the distance along the centre line, projected into the auditorium, from the proscenium line to the front row of seats.

13. Measure the height of eye-level in the front row of seats

in relation to stage-level. It is usual to take 3 ft 8 in. above the floor as eye-level of a seated adult.

14. Measure the distance of the farthest out seats on each side from the centre line, together with the distance along the centre line from the proscenium line.

15. Measure the height, in relation to stage-level, of the highest seat (which will probably be in the back row of the auditorium, and in the highest gallery), and its horizontal distance from the proscenium line.

16. Measure the height above the stage-level, and the horizontal distances from the proscenium and centre lines of all front-of-house lighting equipment.

17. Similarly locate all fixed lighting on stage, and note provision for portable lighting equipment such as dips and socket outlets, booms and perches.

Strictly speaking, the last two sets of measurements do not belong to the category of sightlines, but since you can only see what is lit, lighting is obviously a closely related matter. Some of these measurements will not be of much importance in certain halls. For instance, the highest seat will be of no significance in a hall with a flat floor and no gallery. And, though the data should give a satisfactory description of a theatre with an enclosed stage they apply less and less as the theatre departs from the conventional pattern and finally erupts with an open stage. And differences implicit in the different forms of open stage mean not just another set of measurements but an entirely different approach to scenery and its manipulation altogether.

Sightlines

A designer's concern with sightlines is relatively meaningless if the architect has not first done an adequate job with the auditorium and provision for stage lighting. The word *theatre* comes from a Greek verb meaning *to behold*. And, though it is not of immediate concern to us in this book, the word *auditorium* derives from a Latin word meaning *to hear*. The theatre is a place where the actors can be seen and heard by the audience. If the actors perform on the floor, on the same level as the spectators, the front row will see well, the second row will get an interrupted view, and subsequent rows will see increasingly

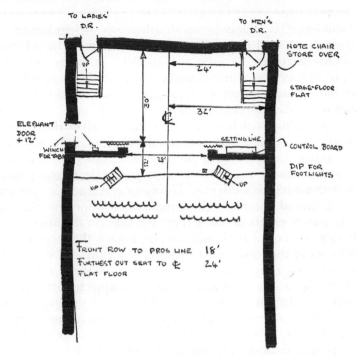

FIG. 10. SKETCH PLAN OF A HALL, WITH ON-THE-SPOT
MEASUREMENTS

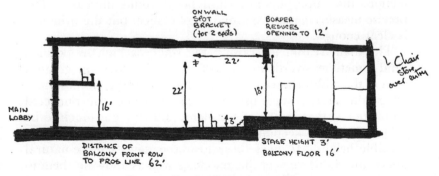

FIG. 11. SKETCH SECTION OF A HALL

less and less. To achieve better sightlines, as ancient history has already discovered for us if we cannot recognize the obvious, it is only necessary to raise the audience in steps, row after row, or to raise the acting area on a stage, or both. Each solution has its advantages and its snags, and history is again useful if we want to examine them.

As the acting area is raised on a stage it gives the actor an increasingly commanding position in relation to the audience. It separates the actor from the audience and puts him in an elevated position. It increases his stature. He is in a position to look down on the audience. He becomes eminent, impressive. These coloured phrases begin to indicate the function of a stage. But in purely practical terms there is a limit to the amount you can raise a stage. It should not be higher than eye-level of spectators in the lowest part of the auditorium. If it is higher than this the front of the stage will gradually cut off lines of sight to the actors who will begin to disappear from the feet upwards as they move away from the front of the stage. Now, as for sightlines, a stage raised to the limit thus imposed may be satisfactory for as many as ten rows, but after this it becomes increasingly difficult for people to see and the rows must therefore be raised. Each row must be raised higher than the one in front of it; there is no sense in simply having a single rise for further rows of seats on the new level. Ideally the further back the row the greater the rise should be, so that, in section, the slope of auditorium floor would increase. The precise measurements are a matter of choice, but the principle is clear enough.

The main reason for raising the stage as high as possible (and sometimes overdoing it, alas) is that it allows the greatest area of the auditorium to be flat. This is desirable in most halls where the auditorium is used for many purposes (unconnected with drama) that require a flat floor. But there is much to be said in favour of keeping the stage-level below maximum permissible height. It gives those near the stage a more natural and comfortable view of the actors, as well as allowing them to see the stage floor. This obviously is more important in a small theatre than a large one. The half-dozen front rows of Covent Garden Opera House get an apalling view; the seats are very expensive and are usually bought by people more anxious to be seen than to see! There are plenty of good seats elsewhere. But these half-dozen rows would accommodate perhaps the entire audience of a small theatre where people go expecting to get their money's worth. In a small theatre bad sightlines mean disaster. And, because we have so many theatres and halls with bad sightlines, the live drama has declined in favour of drama on the vertical screen which is so much easier to place where it can be easily seen, either within the small space of the living room or else high up at one end of an auditorium. For the open stage, where three-dimensional scenery is used, a platform is undesirable; even a chair may obstruct sightlines, and actors will obscure other actors across the stage. There is a lot in favour of an acting area at floor-level, an arena, particularly for the open stage. An arena encourages a relationship between actor and audience that is more natural. To use colourful phrases again, it brings the actor down to the audience's level; it puts actors and audience on an equal footing. Nobody gets unwittingly on to a high horse. But to be practical once more, the different effect of a raised stage and an arena can easily be made the subject of experiment. The results are likely to astonish you, as they have done me on many occasions. Even more important, it is extremely difficult to light actors on a raised stage with the audience on three sides. Light tends to spill excessively into the auditorium. The task becomes virtually impossible with a central stage. Unfortunately the choice does not often lie with the designer who must do the best he can with someone else's theatre. However, he must recognize the possibilities and limitations of the theatre he is going to work in and use the stage to its utmost advantage no matter what its inadequacies.

Designing for the Open Stage

I have given fairly clear guidance for assessing the potentialities of an enclosed stage, but it is not easy to do this for the less common forms of open stage. What follows, then, may become increasingly theoretical, but I hope it will be helpful all the same. As far as scenery is concerned, you can use an open end-stage in much the same way as an enclosed stage, at least for a single setting. Obviously the facilities for changing scenery will not be so generous and will depend on such

equipment as traps, trucks, revolve or elevators as well as
offstage space. Local fire regulations may impose a limit on
how much scenery can be used, and restrict the choice of
materials from which it can be made. This will be mentioned
again later. But an end-stage and a three-sided stage may be
constructed with an architectural background. This is a
permanent structure, related to the whole auditorium and
stage layout, and designed to be used instead of scenery. The
highly developed public playhouses of Tudor times seem to
have made use of elaborate architectural backgrounds. The
Globe theatre of Shakespeare's day may have had, incorporated
in the main structure, a background that included doorways,
an inner stage, a balcony, windows and a gallery above. The
roof over the stage was probably fitted with a winch and pulley
so that a *deus ex machina* could be lowered, and, of course, the
stage floor itself was certainly fitted with a trap. The Mermaid
Theatre in present-day London, the Maddermarket Theatre
in Norwich and the new Festival Theatre at Chichester are all
provided with architectural backgrounds. In most of these the
permanent background can be decorated in different ways, or,
where it is semi-permanent, it can be adapted to suit all sorts
of requirements.

The three-sided stage may have, instead of an architectural
background, facilities for setting up changeable scenery. In
John English's Arena Theatre advantage is taken of space at
the back of the acting area for this purpose. It is of aesthetic
importance to this particular theatre. But clearly if the open
stage uses scenery as background, the factors that govern its
design become increasingly similar to those of the enclosed
stage. No important new problems arise. At the other extreme,
theatre in the round clearly cannot use a scenic or architectural
background at all. But the floor achieves a new significance,
and three-dimensional units of limited height can be used to
compose shapes within a certain volume. This can be made
clear by the most straightforward consideration.

Suppose you are going to arrange the furniture in a room
where the play takes place, say a drawing-room. On an enclosed stage the placing of doorway, fireplace and windows
will be in part determined by offstage space, in part by the
presence of the fourth wall (the proscenium opening), in part

by the focus of communication though the fourth wall and, finally, in part by an appropriate arrangement of the room itself. The same considerations are applied in furnishing the set. There is a tendency for chairs and settee to face the fourth wall, for furniture to be set against any wall except the fourth, and for the fireplaces to be in side walls. In performance actors will be strung out across the stage, more or less facing the audience, even when the situation is supposedly one where people might be expected to form a close group facing, say, the fireplace. Doors, for reasons to be mentioned shortly, will open offstage. This is not stated as an example of good arrangement on any stage, but it is a fair comment on many settings on an enclosed stage.

When the setting is arranged on a central acting area the positions of doors may have to be determined by the actual positions of gangways, but the furniture itself can then be placed with direct reference to appropriateness in reality, tempered by whatever abstract spatial relationships seem useful. This does not mean that it is easy to set a play in theatre in the round, and I have seen enough unsatisfactory settings in this form of theatre to temper any over-enthusiasm I may once have had. My own experience and inclination make me particularly wary of elaborate settings for theatre in the round. Its chief advantage seems to me to be the emphasis it puts on the actors and the play, an advantage that is strengthened by simplicity of setting. But simplicity is in itself a deceptive virtue. Among the opportunities offered by theatre in the round that can be carefully explored by the designer is suspended scenery, ranging from chandeliers to tree branches and transparent shapes; the decoration of the entire auditorium to match the play is a possibility to be considered with an open stage. As already remarked Reinhardt did something of the sort for *The Miracle*, and it can be effective even on a smaller scale.

In a reconnaissance of a theatre with an open stage the designer should measure the acting area, architectural background, revolving stage, trucks, traps and overhead grid—or whatever there is to help him. He should measure and note limits imposed by walls, ceilings and doors and survey the space available for the deployment and storage of scenic units.

Effect of Fire and Safety Regulations on Design

I have often heard it said that fire and safety regulations impose annoying limitations on what can be done in the theatre with scenery and how lighting can be arranged. There is some truth in such remarks and the designer should know how local regulations affect him. To begin with, there is no book of regulations to which you can refer in order to settle a particular point. The Home Office *Manual of Safety Requirements* is mainly concerned with siting and construction of theatres, the arrangements for seating, gangways and exits, the provision of fire-fighting appliances and measures for avoiding panic. Most of this concerns everyone in the theatre, and the designer among the rest. But it does not impose any particular limits on scenery. There is the matter of fire-proofing scenery which is, of course, of real concern to the designer and about which the *Manual* is quite specific. However, the *Manual* gives recommendations and, as far as theatres are concerned (it is different for cinemas), the Chief Fire Officer of the Local Fire Service is wholly responsible for actual rules and his decisions affect what you must or must not do. This is why designers sometimes find they have cause for complaint. There is no uniformity in what can or cannot be done. But most Chief Fire Officers are reasonable men and there is seldom need to come into conflict with them, provided you are reasonable as well!

It is unfortunate that fire regulations are usually the result of disasters in which lives have been lost. Descriptions of theatre fires do not make pleasant reading. The object of regulations is to avoid disasters, and the fact that they do not occur more often is no argument in favour of abandoning precaution. The public has a right to be protected against obvious dangers, quite apart from any feelings of responsibility a sensible theatre manager may have towards persons and property in his care. It is in no one's interests to run unnecessary risks. The most dangerous possibility in the theatre is panic among the audience, for it is this that causes people to be killed when a mishap such as a fire occurs. To avoid panic certain precautions aimed at inspiring confidence in the audience have been devised, including the provision of secondary lighting which must be kept on throughout the performance. As designer and producer I have frequently found secondary

lighting an unmitigated nuisance, particularly when it prevents
a complete blackout in the theatre with an open stage. But
what is nearly always wrong is the design and positions of the
lighting, not the precaution itself.

Panic can be swiftly caused by the sight of fire. And because
of the amount of scenery and lighting apparatus on stage and
the activity on the stage area, it is here that theatre fires have
most often occurred. So it is usually required, in a big theatre
at any rate, that the proscenium wall is fire-resisting, and that
the opening can be filled by a safety curtain. The safety
curtain has two functions; firstly, to conceal the fire on stage
from the audience, secondly, to contain the fire on stage long
enough to allow everyone to leave the theatre. Drenchers and
a lantern light in the stage roof are essential ancillaries to the
safety curtain. Escape from the stage itself is necessary for
artists and staff. It follows that fire-proofing the scenery is a
necessity, and that scenery and furniture must not block up
gangways and exits, nor foul the descent of the safety curtain.
A more complex consideration arises when a large apron stage
juts out beyond the safety curtain into the auditorium. Most
fire authorities will not allow scenery to be set on the auditorium
side of the safety curtain, though scenery made of special
materials—metal and asbestos among them—may be permitted.
A similar restriction is likely to apply to theatres with forms of
open stage where there cannot be a safety curtain. But the
fire risk in a theatre depends a good deal on the amount of
scenery used and stored and is obviously more serious on an
enclosed stage that makes full use of its grid for flying scenery
than on an open stage where a grid is unlikely to be installed
and scenery will probably be minimal. Besides, the risk of
panic decreases in a very small theatre where the exits are
never far away and can easily be reached. As long as the open-
stage theatre takes advantage of such points in its favour, it is
unlikely to cause anxiety and may even be welcomed by the
Fire Chief.

The scene designer should check on local regulations and
find out what concerns him, consulting the Chief Fire Officer if
necessary. He will also make sure that the setting he puts on the
stage is safe and secure. Apart from any immediate damage to
life or limb, a collapse of scenery may be the direct cause of

panic, or it may be a link in the chain of a disaster. Caution
and precaution are always worth taking and, if these are limitations, the designer must accept them.

Theatre Plans

You should now be ready to start on the real business of
designing a set. But I hope that the idea of making a thorough
examination of the theatre appeals to you. It seems to me a
stimulating activity. To make comparisons between theatres
is exciting. It increases your sensitivity to each theatre's
characteristics, and therefore, I hope, helps in the business of
designing settings that belong in the particular theatre. Besides,
it is useful if a designer can be ready to help brief an architect
on making improvements or designing a new theatre. For this
purpose it is not enough to know about one or two theatres.
Although it is impossible to examine every theatre that has ever
been built or planned, the more theatres you do know the
better qualified you may be to choose wisely. Collect photographs and plans of them, pictures of plays in action, designers'
sketches, and descriptions in books and magazines. All theatre
architecture is interesting and has a direct bearing on scenic
design.

In particular, modern and unusual theatres should be taken
into account. Since it is often difficult to find out about
these, it may be worth my listing a few theatres with open
stages, including those already mentioned. If I don't offer you
a list of theatres with enclosed stages it is simply because it
would have to be such a long list. You will have no difficulty
in finding the theatres.

In this country at the time of writing, there are only four
theatres intended for open staging. One of them is in operation
for a small part of the year and another is a converted cinema.
Even the famous Mermaid Theatre was built within the ruined
walls of an old warehouse. It has an open end-stage with an
architectural background. The stage is equipped with a revolve
and this has facilitated the use of scenery. However, limitations
are imposed on the choice of scenic materials by regulations for
fire-prevention. The Mermaid has interesting antecedents,
and the story of Bernard Miles's progress from a preoccupation
with the Elizabethan theatre to this particular modern building

is an interesting one. The Festival Theatre at Chichester has a three-sided open stage. It is a large theatre, but the use of scenery on open stages, even in large theatres, is within our present scope. This theatre has an architectural background which can be taken down, so that scenic structures can be erected instead. Backstage space is extremely limited. The Victoria Theatre in Stoke-on-Trent is a theatre in the round converted from an old cinema. It is extremely simple and uses virtually no scenery whatever. Finally, there is the little Traverse Theatre in Edinburgh, with a central stage and the audience on two opposite sides. It is a modest and ingenious conversion of unlikely premises.

In addition to these four theatres, the Assembly Hall in Edinburgh is usually converted into a three-sided open stage during the Festival, and, from time to time, companies on the famous "fringe" make use of open stage techniques. John English's Arena Theatre travels from Birmingham, where it sets up under canvas in Cannon Hill Park during the summer, to Cardiff and to Newcastle upon Tyne. The Arena Theatre has a three-sided open stage, with a scenic background. The stage can be enveloped by a curtain. Another travelling open-stage theatre is my own Studio Theatre which sets up a theatre in the round in halls, for instance, at Hemel Hempstead, Dartington Hall, and in the Library at Scarborough. Once again this theatre in the round is of extreme simplicity and uses very little scenery. As far as I know there are no other professional companies using forms of open stage, but an increasing number of amateur and educational groups are using all sorts of halls and unlikely places as theatres for occasional open-stage productions. The Questors and L.A.M.D.A. theatres are both highly flexible and will provide several different forms of open stage as well as an enclosed stage. The new Nottingham Playhouse can be adapted for open-stage work. There are other plans. But they are only plans at present.

In the United States the situation is very different. There are so many open-stage theatres that it is difficult to make a selection. I have arbitrarily listed most of those I visited when I was last in America. First of all a theatre in the round of large size (a seating capacity of 2,000) with a raised stage can be seen in the shape of a geodesic dome glowing silver and gold, at Fort Worth in Texas. This is the Casa Mañana Theatre. Its productions are usually musical shows and light operas. Musical entertainment can be seen in many of the tent theatres which are temporarily put up in the summer in different parts of the States. Such theatres have orchestra pits to one side of the central stage.

By contrast, the Tufts Arena Theatre is very small indeed, and has been converted from an old gymnasium. It is a theatre in the round, used by students of Tufts College at Medford, Massachusetts, and there is a continuous series of productions covering a wide range of dramatic literature. This is one of the most intimate and exciting little theatres I have ever seen. In spite of its small size, productions frequently make use of scenic pieces. Another theatre in the round where scenery has been interestingly used is the Alley Theatre in Houston, Texas. I shall say something about a production there later (page 106). Here again, the theatre has been made from an old building. But in the same town, the Playhouse is a specially built theatre in the round, one of the few that I have seen with an auditorium that is actually round. It has a revolving acting area.

The unexpectedly named Drury Lane Theatre has a central raised stage, and the theatre is advantageously placed immediately beneath a large and very smart restaurant in the suburbs of Chicago. In Washington, D.C., the Arena Theatre, again a theatre in the round, has a splendid new building. The acting area is trapped and there is flying space overhead, making a variety of scenic effects possible. At the University of Washington in Seattle is the first of America's specially built theatres in the round. It is very small, and very simple, though some scenery is used.

The Charles Street Playhouse in Boston, Massachusetts, has a three-sided stage with a scenic background. It is converted from an old chapel. The Oregon Shakespeare Festival at Ashland is held in a reconstruction of the sort of theatre that we guess Shakespeare might have written for. There are several such theatres in the States. They tend to put too much emphasis, for my liking, on whitewash and black beams, on the supposed inner stage and balcony above, but disregard the actual actor-audience relationships that seem to me to be so important. At Ashland the rows of seats are arranged very much as in a conventional enclosed-stage theatre. But the attempt, however compromised, is well worth seeing.

In Canada there is Sir Tyrone Guthrie's world-famous Shakespeare Festival Theatre. It has a three-sided open stage

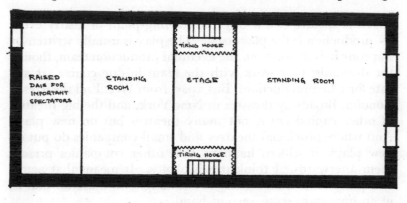

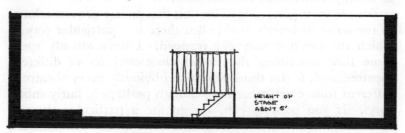

FIG. 12. TRANSVERSE STAGE
Plan and section showing the idea of an Elizabethan stage, suggested by
Leslie Hotson's book, *Shakespeare's Wooden O*

with an architectural background. In Europe there is the interesting Théâtre en rond in Paris, and in Milan the Teatro Sant' Erasmo, which has a transverse arena, recalling Professor Leslie Hotson's researches in his book *Shakespeare's Wooden O*. If this seems a slender harvest of open stages in Europe, remember that on the continent you can find innumerable enclosed stages dating from the Renaissance to the present day, and many of them glorious by any comparison in the world. They'll occupy all your time!

IV

GET TO KNOW THE PLAY

IN the theatre of our day the starting-point of nearly every
production is the play itself. The play is usually written by
someone in isolation from the eventual production team, though
the dramatist may work with the team in due course, at any
rate for a first production. But apart from West End theatres in
London, Broadway theatres in New York, and the big theatres
of other capital cities, not many theatres put on new plays.
And where provincial theatres and small companies do put on
new plays, it seldom happens that other companies present
them afterwards. I think this is a pity. It means that actors
and producers and designers are dealing with material that is,
in an important sense, second-hand.

For the most part, my feelings on this matter are not related
to the scene designer's work. But there is a particular way in
which the designer may get trapped. I have already spent
some time describing the broad characteristics of different
theatres, and, if you think about it, obviously every theatre is
different from every other one, though perhaps in fairly subtle
ways. If you possibly can, design for a particular theatre.
Your only excuse for not doing so is if the theatre has not been
chosen (as may happen to a West End designer) or if the play
is to make an extensive tour, calling at many theatres of very
different types and without any proper home.

It is important to remember that any stage plans and photographs of settings that may accompany a published play were
made for a certain theatre, and probably not yours at that.
There is no sense in copying. I have seen many productions of
Sailor Beware by small companies in small theatres where an
attempt at copying the London setting has been made. In
London there was a large stage and the extra furniture that
had to be introduced into the play in order to fill the space was,
perhaps, justified. To cram all that unwanted furniture into a
small space is absurd and makes acting become an obstacle
race. The scene is meant to be a working-class parlour. The

size of the room on the London stage was incredible. For this
play, a smaller stage has positive advantages. Why not take
them? Besides, most designers who fall into the trap of copying
someone else's designs are bad designers, and there is no design
worse than a bad second-hand design!

The Play as a Stimulus to Design

Once the play has been chosen, everyone gets to work. The
cast rehearses with the producer. The designer gets down to
details. Everyone reads the play, of course. It is a good idea
for the designer to get immersed in it, to know it inside out
and backwards. You will quickly ascertain the practical
demands made by the play. There may be one set, or a number
of settings. If there is more than one setting the designs must
not only relate to each other but be planned to make use of
whatever scene-shifting facilities are available in the theatre.
A setting will make a number of clear presentational demands
according to the place where the action occurs, the historical
period, and the general mood manifest in the author's attitude
to his material. Let us take an example.

In the published edition of *The Birthday Party* by Harold
Pinter, the play begins with the following description of the
setting—

> The living-room of a house in a seaside town. Door leading to hall
> D.L. Back door and small window U.L. Kitchen hatch centre back.
> Kitchen door U.R. Table and chairs centre. Two ordinary chairs above
> and left of table, one armchair right of table. Sideboard above small
> fireplace on right wall. Stool and wooden box for shoe brushes in
> fireplace.

This is quite specific. The synopsis of acts shows that there is
no change of setting. After reading the play through you will
quickly see that it is a modern play taking place in the present
day. However, I make an immediate reservation about all this.
It is important to know that this is the living-room of a house
in a seaside town. We might have gathered as much from the
play itself, but it is useful to be told right away. There is a door
leading to the hall. Yes, it is used in the play and might be
expected anyhow. How important is it that this door should be
down left? How important are the precise positions indicated
for other doors, window, fireplace and furniture? In the

description that opens almost every play, you will find such
precise directions. More often they describe the original
setting used, as noted by the stage manager, than represent the
author's expectations. For this reason they can be taken with
a grain of salt. Don't abandon them deliberately without
reading the play.

A few writers, including George Bernard Shaw and James
Barrie, have carefully written the published directions themselves. They put in such detailed description mainly for the
armchair reader at a time when reading novels was a more
respectable pastime than going to the theatre. Directions of
this sort were never intended to be followed slavishly in production. Anyhow, no author outside your own company can
anticipate the particular conditions under which you must
work. It is right and proper to take note of stage directions,
and decide for yourself how exactly they represent the author's
demands, or what would be the author's demands if he knew
your theatre and the circumstances of the production. It may
help if I add that when Harold Pinter produced *The Birthday
Party* himself for my own theatre-in-the-round company, he used
a very different setting from the one just described. It was not
necessarily a better setting in any way—I designed it—but the
conditions under which the production was done demanded
something quite different from the original (*see* Fig. 43, page 104).

But having read *The Birthday Party* once or more you will
find that there are matters more important than the positions
of doorways. The play uses the language of reality. In some
ways the language is positively photographic, it is so true to life,
but in others it is poetic. There are repetitions that take on a
hypnotic quality—usually of a hilarious or horrific sort. The
play is wildly funny, and absolutely terrifying. An important
scene takes place in the dark, with the occasional stabbing
illumination of the beam from a torch. Yet we are in a seaside
town. Sun, perhaps, is what we should think of. The play is
one of schizoid contrasts, or so it seems to me. The living-room
of a house in a seaside town? This is a living-room with a
difference! There is no sense in putting a box set on stage, with
doors and windows in appropriate places, and then doing a
nice job of interior decoration. Though, come to think of it,
the house might have been nice once. . . .Well, read the play

a few more times and see what ideas begin to take shape in your mind. You should gradually perceive how to use the space at your disposal, the size of the acting area, the height of the scenery, the shape of the setting, the value of lines, curves, angles, symmetry, irregularity; how to use colour, texture, decorative detail, style. The stimulus, I suggest, comes from reading the play. The choice of elements in the visual interpretation comes from the designer. The ability to choose well is the hall-mark of the artist. Practice sharpens your skill, knowledge gives you a wide range to choose from, but only natural talent can make your choice both original and good.

South is a play of tremendous atmospheric strength. The relationships between the characters seem to be complex, but in fact they are various facets of a strong, central theme. The play turns out to have an almost classical simplicity. It has also an almost classical power. This is admirably reflected in the first sketch (Plate III) for the setting, designed by Disley Jones. The model of the set, and the photograph (Plate IV) showing the final setting on stage, show differences of detail, but clearly the designer felt the impact of the play and saw exactly how he wanted to translate it into the visual terms of scenic background. Notice how the sketch gives a fairly accurate indication of the eventual appearance of the scenery itself.

Relationship between Designer and Producer

The designer may work this far alone. But the producer will want to have a say in the arrangement of the ground-plan. He may also have ideas, more or less definite, about interpretive elements in the design. Or he may rely entirely on his designer. The relationship between the two people is highly personal, and it is seldom the same between different individuals. It is an important relationship, and the designer should take pains to find out the best way of working with his producer, in order to get the best possible results on stage. And no matter how little the producer knows about scenery, consultation between the two may be helpful to both and it is certainly necessary for an integrated production.

Some producers have no visual imagination whatever. Their main qualification may be the understanding of the play,

particularly of a classical play that requires academic scholarship. Some producers on the other hand know more about
design than the designer and visualize the whole production
from the word go! Give and take is necessary. The designer
is not often so closely concerned with the actors. But they are
the people who will use the set. Some actors like to stand well
clear of scenery, as though they were afraid the flats would fall
down on them. Perhaps they have learned from experience?
Others may enjoy a setting that gives them a chance to lean on
something, clamber, climb over, or mount to a great height.
Some actors treat scenery gracefully. Others knock it over given
half a chance. It is worth knowing about idiosyncrasies of this
sort.

When I was producer at Lowestoft repertory theatre, years
ago, Tom Lingwood was the designer. He had the knack of
being able to use his own original ideas in relation to the rest
of the company. Our young leading actor, John Neville, was
keenly interested in each set design, to see how it could best
be used in action. In one play it might be a question of
furniture (as when John Neville played Roland Maule in
Present Laughter) and the available space between a settee and
a chair. In another play, *The Eagle Has Two Heads*, in which
John Neville played Stanislas, there is an important window
through which the character makes his first entrance, and, in
the final scene, the stage direction reads—

> Stanislas rushes forward and bounds up the stairs to the Queen's side.
> The poison grips him. The Queen falls bringing down one of the curtains.
> The Queen dies. Stanislas falls backwards, rolling down the entire
> staircase and dies at the bottom.

The play is the sort that benefits from close co-operation
between all concerned with the production, as you can see.
Tom Lingwood not only enjoyed this sort of co-operation, but
in this particular play he brought off one of his cleverest tricks
with perspective. We wanted to make the maximum use of the
smallish acting area. The play requires two settings, the second
of which must have the solid staircase referred to, while the
first scene is in the Queen's bedroom—supposedly an enormous
room. The first setting was erected inside the second. The
bed occupied the centre of the back wall. It looked big, and

The Paint Shop at the Little Theatre, Lewes

PLATE I

Sᴇᴀɴ Kᴇɴɴʏ's Sᴇᴛᴛɪɴɢ ꜰᴏʀ *Oliver* ᴀᴛ ᴛʜᴇ Nᴇᴡ Tʜᴇᴀᴛʀᴇ,
Lᴏɴᴅᴏɴ

PLATE II

SKETCH BY DISLEY JONES FOR THE SET OF *South* AT THE LYRIC
THEATRE, HAMMERSMITH

A design takes shape from a sketch, through ground-plans (*see* Fig. 46),
to a model. The sketch above is by the designer Disley Jones for *South*
by Julian Green at the Lyric Theatre, Hammersmith. Next comes a
model (Plate IV), then constructional drawings (*see* Fig. 47). Finally,
the setting is put on the stage. Alterations and adjustments may be
introduced at any moment, but the basic idea here remains the same
throughout. The finished setting is shown in Plate IV (*lower*)

PLATE III

South—MODEL OF THE SET

PLATE IV

South—THE ACTUAL SET

achieved its deceptive appearance of size by being built in perspective.

Choice of Style of Interpretation

The play is the starting-point from which nearly all the designer's ideas will spring. We have considered practical and presentational requirements, and listed the directions in which interpretation will move. The play will suggest a particular style of visual interpretation. The setting that begins to take shape in your mind as you read *The Birthday Party* will be quite different from the same writer's *The Caretaker*. The difference lies in more than the *milieu* in which each play is set. It is a question of the author's attitude to his material, which must be reflected in the designer's attitude to the same material. Style may be best explored by looking at many different styles of scenic presentation. This is an idea that is comparatively new. In the past, the artist simply designed the settings in the only style that was known—to him and to everyone else. It was the right way, the only way. But today, we do not subscribe to the idea of a single right way, and with the aid of historical approach, and knowledge of the immense diversity of designing techniques, we can make a considerable degree of choice. The limit to our choice is often simply the limit of our skill, but sometimes it is the deliberate rejection of convention in favour of a purely personal style.

There is no need to follow any style if you wish to be entirely original. But choose or not, scenic styles in our day seem to range between two extremes of purpose. On the one hand, there is the scenery that strives to give the appearance of reality. A living-room setting for instance may be designed and painted with reference to the appearance of the actual proportions, shapes, colours and so on of walls and ceilings. And the furniture in the setting is simply real furniture. The effect might not be convincing if real wallpaper were used, since the audience is not in the position of a real observer in the room, and, as we have already said, it is the appearance to the audience that must echo reality. On the other hand, there is scenery of theatrical convention—scenery that is scenery and everyone knows it.

No matter how hard the designer tries to achieve reality, no

adult in the audience should be deceived. It is a different
matter with children whose sense of reality transcends adult
distinctions. And scenery of convention always catches some
degree of illusion. When, on the oriental stage, a huge flag is
waved across the floor as a symbol for the sea it catches one's
imagination. One believes in the convention. These extremes
of purpose can never be completely separated, and every
creative artist in the theatre deals with each of them, putting
the emphasis further one way or the other. Nearly every
generation applauds its new actors for their naturalness. The
actors of the last generation were false, unnatural—they over-
acted, they were ham. So Burbage was hailed and rejected,
and Betterton and Kean and Kemble and Irving. Each
generation chooses its own position in the scale between reality
and convention, and this is reflected by actors, writers and
designers. Our own generation seems unwilling to commit
itself and an immense variety of styles is acceptable to the
public—perhaps this is saying no more than that our theatre
is out of fashion or between fashions.

V

MAKING SCENERY

WHEN the designer has absorbed the play, he usually starts
to make sketches of the setting. This is one of the most
exciting phases of the designer's work—working out the actual
designs, adjusting them, elaborating, simplifying or starting
again. A sketch can be swiftly made and approved or rejected
in favour of another sketch and yet another. Some designers do
their sketch work in a drawing-book, using only a pencil. You
can also use a pen, water-colour or pastels. Any scrap of paper
such as the back of an envelope will do for a start when you are
working the design out. I enjoy sketching in heavy pencil on
newspaper—of which there is nearly always some at hand, but
you may choose good art paper or board for your final sketches.
Most designers sketch a setting as it will appear from the
auditorium, and a good ground-plan shows the way the design
is put on to the stage. When the sketches are clear and ready,
the designer shows them to producer and gets his approval,
comments or requests for new sketches. This is a crucial matter.
It is important that the designer should be able to convey in a
sketch his real intentions so that the producer can appreciate
them, and so that the final setting bears a close relationship to
the original sketch. But there is another moment when the
designer can check with the producer. We'll come to this
shortly.

Plans and Drawings

When the sketches have been approved and decided on, the
designer sets about making plans and working drawings. At
least, he should do so if he is going to have new flats made for
the production. But for some reason or another you may reject
the full process—either because the circumstances are special,
or you are working with a stock of ready-made scenery, or
because you are too skilled or too lazy to be conscientious.
When there is a fixed and limited stock of scenery to be used, a
complete set of working drawings is not necessary. But when

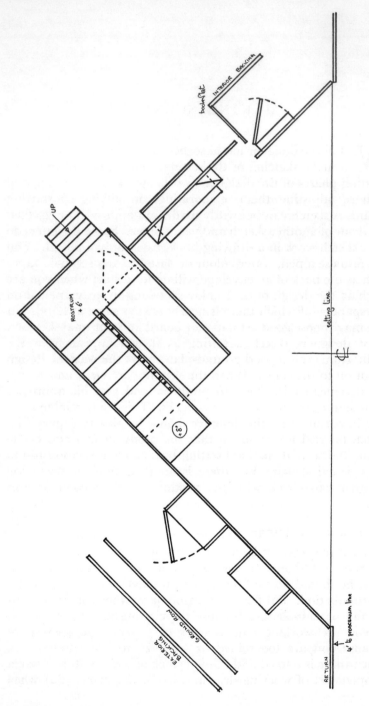

FIG. 13. GROUND-PLAN OF A SET

such drawings are required they are made on a drawing-board,
using draughtsman's equipment. The first drawing is an accurate ground-plan. This will show both the setting and how
it fits on to the stage for which it is designed. The data referred
to in Chapter III come in useful here. The plan is drawn to
scale, usually one-quarter of an inch to one foot, and shows the
correct shape and size of the setting in relation to the proscenium and centre lines, it shows the position and angle of
every flat, the width of doors, the way they open, the positions
and size of windows, fireplaces, pillars, alcoves and other
architectural detail. All backings will be shown in position.
Surrounding space will also be shown so that access and storage
can be confirmed, as well as the positioning of extra lighting
for backings, cloths and so on.

It is a good idea to make a ground-plan on draughtsman's
tracing paper so that copies can easily be run off by dye-line or
other duplicating process. The ground-plan is used by all sorts
of people; by the producer for working out the production
scheme, by the stage manager for plotting the setting-up
schedule; by the lighting designer; by the stage staff; by the
technicians who build the set. It is a good idea to have a
number of copies and to make sure that the plan is absolutely
accurate.

The second drawing to make is a vertical section. This
serves to check sightlines and the arrangement of borders, the
distribution of lines from the grid, and the position of lighting
bars. It must be an accurate drawing, and should show the
sightlines from the front row and from the highest seat. The
position of the highest seat itself need not be included on
the drawing—this would either make it very big or reduce the
scale unnecessarily. The angles from the highest seat can be
worked out trigonometrically or drawn independently and
measured with a protractor for transference to the vertical
sightline drawing. The proscenium opening and, more important, the teaser should be shown, together with all platforms
and levels and openings in the setting. The sightlines, drawn
from the extreme seats past the teaser, will show where borders
are necessary and how much of the setting can be seen, how
tall backings should be, and whether the actors can be seen on
raised levels. For horizontal sightlines, the ground-plan can be

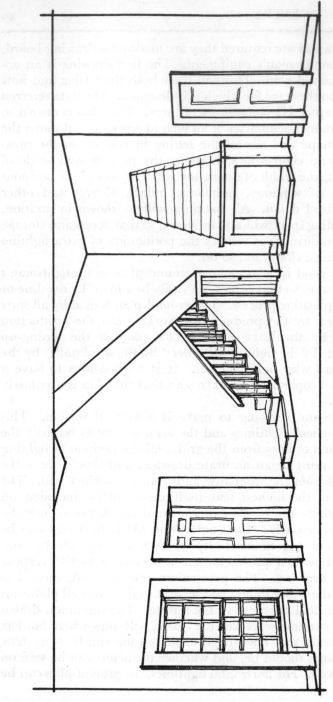

FIG. 14. PERSPECTIVE OF A SET

used in the same way provided that the extreme seats and the proscenium opening, together with returns and tormentors, are drawn in. But a separate and simpler plan may be drawn on a smaller scale just for the purpose of checking horizontal sightlines. By checking sightlines the designer will determine if the

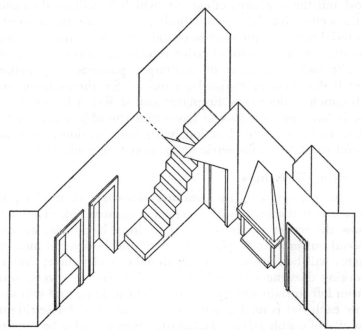

FIG. 15. AXONOMETRIC PROJECTION OF A SET

set is satisfactory. Adjustment may be necessary to the setting or to borders, teaser, and returns. In many theatres, including some of the best West End theatres, sightlines from the extreme side seats are bad, and much of the setting as well as much of the acting area is cut off from sight. Seats in the gallery often give bad sightlines to the setting because backcloths and back walls are more or less obscured and sometimes even the front of the stage. In all honesty such seats should not be sold to the public without warning. Whatever happens, the designer must not make matters worse.

The third drawing should be a front elevation of the setting itself. Once again, the drawing must be made accurately, to scale. It represents a front view of the setting spread out in a single plane. Vertical and horizontal measurements of all flats and cloths can be checked. Laid out in this way, the drawing enables the designer to check the doors and windows and other architectural features in relation to wall area, to work out the total area of canvas (which he will need to know if the scenery is to be specially built), to calculate the amount of material necessary for window curtains and other wall hangings, to estimate the amount of paint required and organize design details such as repeats of wallpaper patterns or panelling. Detail drawings may also be required for three-dimensional units such as doorways, fireplaces and stairs; a larger scale is used—say one inch to one foot—and the object is drawn in plan, front and side elevation, with some sections. It is also useful to make an isometric or axonometric projection.

Working Drawings

Now we come to the working drawings themselves, the drawings that show how the scenery is constructed. They must show the scenery as it is looked at from backstage, in scale, spread out in a single plan. Vertical and horizontal measurements will be shown, as in the designer's elevation; but the working drawing will be laid out, of course, in reverse order (from left to right instead of from right to left), and will show how each flat is made, how flats are furnished for setting-up, the size of openings, etc. Detail drawings will also be required for any new stage machinery, such as traps, trucks, revolves and elevators, and it is useful to make drawings to show special rigging or setting-up techniques—especially the rigging of irregular ceiling pieces, the bracing of cut-outs and the jacking of big three-dimensional units.

These drawings serve to show how the set should be put together and constructed, to check that it will fit in with the theatre sightlines, and to give the production team and stage staff an idea of what is coming. A further drawing can be made with the help of the ground-plan and elevation: this is an accurate perspective, showing exactly how the setting will look from a particular seat in the auditorium. Not many designers in this country bother with a perspective, but it is obviously extremely useful, particularly for checking with the producer.

American designers nearly always make perspectives, very well too. If you look at the perspective drawn by Jo Mielziner for *Death of a Salesman* and compare it with a photograph of the actual setting, the similarity is uncanny. But this is as it should be—and we should expect nothing less from so experienced and expert a designer.

Making Flats and Cloths

So much for drawings. The designer's next job is to get on with painting the settings. But somebody has got to make the flats, and, although in many provincial repertory theatres and little theatres there will already be a complete stock of flats and cloths, while in other theatres the management will order new flats from scenic suppliers, the designer in a small theatre may have to make his own. There is certainly no harm in knowing how it is done, and a brief summary of scene building for beginners seems appropriate here.

Scenery is usually made up of flats and cloths. Flats for the stage are made of canvas stretched on a timber framework; in television and film studios, flats are more often made of plywood or hardboard, but this is usually framed in much the same way as theatrical canvas and I shall not make any further reference to its use. Timber framework is 3 in. × 1 in. planed deal, of a grade with few knots in it. Each theatre usually has a standard height for flats, and this should be taken into consideration when lengths of timber are ordered. The framework of a plain flat is made up of two vertical pieces called stiles, and horizontal pieces called rails; there may be three rails to a flat, and the middle one is called a toggle rail. It is usual to put corner braces, called battens, across diametrically opposed corners. There are several different ways of making the joints. Professionally this is done by a machine, with mortise and tenon joins at each corner, while the toggle rails are let into shoes. A simpler method is to use a halved joint, which should be clear from the drawing, and simplest of all the butt joint. These can be easily made by hand. Butt joins are strengthened by using corrugated dogs and metal, plywood or hardboard corner plates. Slightly more expensive, but very easy for the amateur to cope with, is the join made with shaped metal shoes which are specially designed for each of the different joints on a flat. The wood must be measured in relation to whichever join is to be done. And note, when using butt joins, that the rails at the top and bottom of the flat always extend to the full width of the flat, otherwise the stile might split when running a flat during setting-up or scene-changing.

The framework must now be covered. There are various sorts of material to be had for this purpose ranging from a

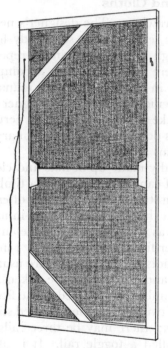

FIG. 16. SKETCH OF A PLAIN FLAT, ABOUT TEN FEET HIGH,
BACK VIEW

cheap common quality 10-oz hessian to a good fire-proofed flax scenic canvas (which will be about three times as expensive), or 8-oz cotton duck for about the same price. Scenic canvases are usually best to use as they work and last well. They are usually available in 72-in. width but may also be supplied 36-in. and other widths. Having obtained your canvas, you now need scissors, a hammer, tacks, hot glue and a trimming knife. First, cut a length of canvas of the appropriate width so that it precisely covers the framework. Now tack the canvas to one

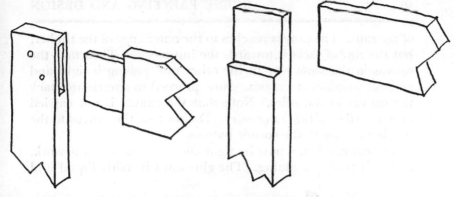

FIG. 17. MORTISE AND TENON JOIN   FIG. 18. HALVED JOIN

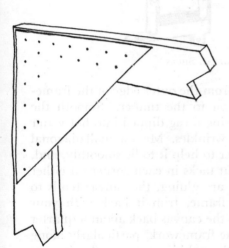

FIG. 19. CORNER PIECES OF HARDBOARD OR
PLYWOOD FOR STRENGTHENING A BUTT JOIN

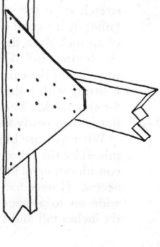

FIG. 20. STRENGTHENING PIECE ON A TOGGLE RAIL

55

of the rails. The canvas reaches to the outer edge of the timber, but the row of tacks is towards the inner edge. Then tack the canvas in the same way to the other rail, pulling it tight and without wrinkles or creases. Now proceed to stretch and tack the canvas to the stiles. Note that the canvas is not carried over the edge of the framework. Do not tack the canvas to the toggle rail, nor to the corner battens.

The canvas should now be tight and even on the framework, and it is ready for gluing. The glue must be fairly liquid and

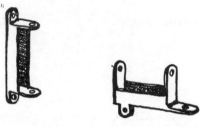

FIG. 21. METAL SHOES

hot. Folding back the canvas from the outer edge of the framework, brush the glue evenly on to the timber. Smooth the canvas down on to the glue, using a rag dipped into hot water and wrung out. Avoid making wrinkles. Make a small diagonal cut in the canvas at each corner to help it to lie smoothly, and, when the gluing is finished, put tacks in each corner on either side of the cut. If, when you are gluing, the canvas tends to stretch over the edge of the frame, trim it back with your knife; it is a good idea to keep the canvas back about a quarter of an inch from the edge of the framework, particularly along the bottom rail which takes the rubbing when a flat is run; the edge of the canvas is bent into the framework by trimming it firmly with a sharp knife. A Stanley trimming knife is ideal for this work. The glue will take a few hours to dry and the flat is then ready for painting.

When you are building up a stock of flats, the height is determined by the proscenium opening, and the different widths by considerations of utility, and limitations that may be imposed by access. (I once had to help get a set that included flats six feet wide on to a stage that had only one access door—five feet six inches tall and two feet six inches wide!)

Canvas comes in certain widths, seventy-two inches wide is most common. A flat any wider than this is likely to be difficult to handle. When designing narrower flats, wastage of

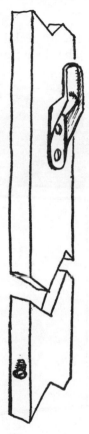

FIG. 22. LASHING CLEAT AND TYING-OFF SCREW

canvas should be avoided by building two flats three feet wide or one two feet and one four feet wide and so on.

Flats are furnished with fittings to enable them to be lashed together easily. When viewed from the back, each flat is equipped with a lashline in the stile on one side. This can conveniently be made of sash cord. It should be secured through a hole near the top of the stile. Cleats should be provided on both stiles. The heights of all furniture should be standard on every flat, and the lashline should be just clear of the floor when hanging free. The sketches show the arrangement clearly.

Door Flats

Door flats are built with a special opening that is secured at the bottom by a sill. The door frame itself is best prepared

FIG. 23. DOOR FLAT

separately and secured in this opening. Windows and fireplaces can be treated in a similar way. By using canvas panels it is easy to make a door flat serve as window or fireplace flat, or the window and fireplace units can themselves be made to fill the entire opening. Fireplaces on a grand scale can simply be placed against an ordinary flat. A canvas panel, or header, can be used in conjuction with standard flats to make a large doorway or archway.

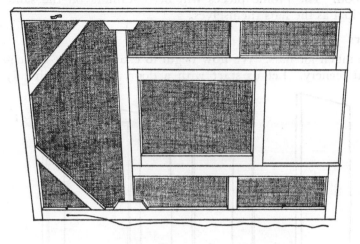

Fig. 25. Door Flat, with Filling Piece, can be used for Fireplaces

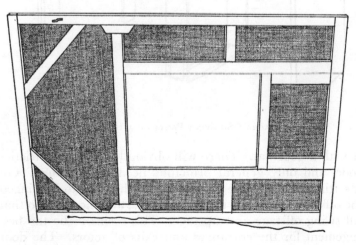

Fig. 24. Door Flat, with Filling Piece, can be used as a Window Flat

Irregular flats, such as ground rows, are made by taking stock flats and adding profile pieces cut out of hardboard or plywood. The profile pieces will need framing on the same principal as the flats themselves.

Doors

So much for flats. We now begin to examine three-dimensional scenery. Let us start with a door. We have already

FIG. 26. DIAGRAM SHOWING PARTS OF A SCENIC DOOR

dealt with a door flat. There will obviously be many varieties of door, and only general principles need be explained. On most settings it is sensible to arrange for the door to be hinged on the offstage side of the thickness pieces, and mounted so that it will swing offstage and upstage. This seems to be the best arrangement for the entrances and exits of actors. The door does not interfere with on-stage space. When open it serves in part as a backing, and when closed it allows the thickness pieces to remain in sight. Since only one side of the door is seen it can be simply built and painted. But the arrangement is arbitrary, and, when you know what you're doing, choose for yourself exactly what to do!

The thickness of the door frame can be made of 4-in. × 1-in. timber. The casing, made of the same timber, should be

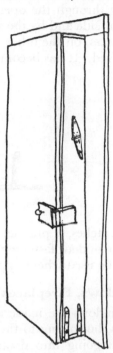

FIG. 27. DIAGRAM INDICATING ASSEMBLY OF A SCENIC DOOR

FIG. 28. BACK VIEW OF ASSEMBLED DOOR

The flap-hinge drops down when the door is in its flat

screwed to the front of the thickness. Sill irons must be secured across the base of the thickness pieces, and strap hinges put in place for securing the doorway—though this may be left until it is in place.

The door itself should be made of a framework consisting of two stiles, two rails and a centre toggle. This framework should be made of 4-in. × 1-in., and assembled as for a flat. It should be covered by plywood or hardboard, firmly glued and nailed in place. The door is hinged to the thickness by strap hinges, bent as needed.

When you are constructing a door, measurements should be worked out in relation to the design of the setting and to the size of the door flat, if it already exists. The thickness frame, including the securing strap hinges, should be able to pass freely through the opening. It is held in place by the casing on one side and by the strap hinges, which drop down from the thickness, on the other. Door furniture can be put in place as required. It has become common to secure all stage doors with

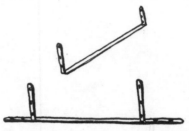

FIG. 29. SILL IRONS FOR DOORWAYS

ball catches, a practice that I find entirely meaningless. The choice of door fastening should be made carefully. A rim latch may be used where appropriate.

Windows, Fireplaces and Rostrums

Windows are made and secured in much the same way as doors, but owing to the immense variety of structures it is not worth going into details. It is not usual to use glass, and glazing bars can be made of plain timber. It is unnecessary to use proper counterweight systems for sash windows. These can be held in place by friction alone, by plugs of thin dowel (or a nail) through the frame, or by friction springs.

Fireplaces can usually be obtained from a demolition contractor's yard. They are usually heavy, but can be adapted to secure to a door flat quite easily. Alternatively, the fireplace can be designed and made specially for the setting. A small screen will be needed to fill in the fireplace opening.

The most useful form of three-dimensional scenery enables us to provide different acting levels. Rostrums can be made either rigid or folding. The rigid platform is easier to make, and less expensive, but it is heavier and occupies more storage space than a folding platform. A folding platform is not usually

so robust, and it may be noisy in use when it has to withstand
the vigorous movement of actors over it.

When making a rigid platform, start with the outside frame.
This should be made of 1-in. × 4-in. or larger timber, depending on the overall size of the platform. The framing members
must be placed on edge and butt joined with nails. The corners

FIG. 30. SCENIC WINDOW

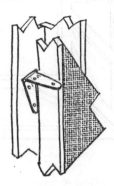

FIG. 31. SKETCH TO SHOW STRAP-
HINGE OF DOOR OR WINDOW
HOLDING AGAINST ITS FLAT

should be reinforced with strap irons. Inside supporting
members should run parallel with the length of the platform, at
distances of not less than two feet apart. The top of the platform
can be made of flooring timber or blockboard, nailed or screwed
in place. The top of the platform is usually padded with felt,
and covered with canvas that is carried down over the side of
the frame where it is tacked and glued in place; 2-in. × 4-in.
legs can be bolted to the inside corners of the frame with
carriage bolts. The legs can be made in sets of different lengths,
but for any height of over one foot, they should be braced by
diagonal lengths of 3-in. × 1-in.

Folding platforms, or parallels, are expensive to build and it is
worth working to a module so that they can be used in different
relationships to each other. They must be made with accuracy,
using good mortise and tenon joins.

There are two sorts of folding platform. Both have removable tops, and frames that can be folded, and the difference

lies in the way the framework, or base, is folded. The framework of the standard parallel is in one piece, and it has the advantage of being more easily shifted. The continental

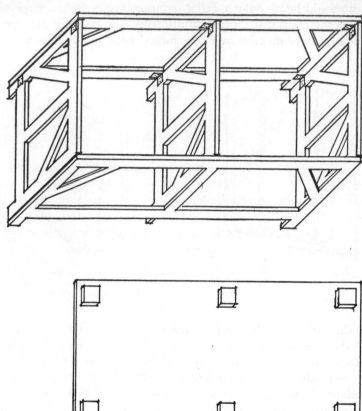

Fig. 32. Standard Parallel or Rostrum: Axonometric Projection

parallel has removable centre supports. These do not interfere with the folding of the outside frames which can, therefore, be arranged to fold inwards so that there is no increase in length when they are folded. Further, the continental parallel can have interior supports placed closely together, and as many as required. Thus the platform can conveniently be built of a much larger size.

The continental parallel is made with an outside framework in four sections. The end frames are halved and hinged to fold inside the side frames. The centre frames slide into place between the pairs of battens that are screwed to the side frames, and they are fitted with countersunk strap-iron hooks that engage in notches in the side frames.

The standard parallel has a framework that folds in one piece, and the distance between the end frame and the centre support must be not less than the width of the platform, otherwise the support would foul the outside frame and prevent compact folding. This imposes a limitation of overall size. For reasons of structural safety, a standard parallel should not be more than three feet wide.

Rostrum tops may be made of floor-boards battened together underneath, or of blockboard. When the top is in position, these battens, or special locating pieces on the blockboard should hold the top locked to the framework, which is thus prevented from folding by mistake. The top should be padded and covered with canvas that is pulled over the edge and tacked and glued underneath.

There is another way of making rostrums. A skeleton may be constructed of slotted angle or tubular scaffolding and floorboards or blockboard secured on top. These are not folding platforms, nor are they exactly permanent. Their advantages are that they can be strongly made, of any size and shape, that the skeleton can be taken to pieces when the rostrum is finished with and the members used again for quite a different structure. There are two main difficulties; slotted angle and tubular scaffoldings are expensive, particularly if you want to take advantage of the relative lightness of alloy metal. And engineering know-how is essential if the rostrums are to be safe and steady.

Other Units

There are a number of ways in which irregular units such as steps, pillars, trees and rocks can be made. The traditional material for framework is timber, with irregular faces of wire netting covered by canvas or papiermâché. New facing materials such as phenolic foam and Fibreglass are beginning to become known and it cannot be long before a number of plastic materials are available for this purpose. Slotted angle and tubular scaffolding may be used for skeleton members. I have made use of Dexion slotted angle for all sorts of purposes and find it extremely versatile. When I have used tubular scaffolding, Gascoigne Kee Klamps have provided admirable joining members. If you can get to know these materials you will quickly see that they have immense possibilities.

Always remember that scenery for the stage will probably have to be light in weight, of a size easy to move, structurally sound and fire-proof. In film and television studios weight and size are not necessarily important—though the other considerations, of course, are. Film scenery is often made very solidly and relief work for both regular and irregular surfaces may be made of plaster. Film studio plasterers can be relied on to do expert and ingenious work. But plasterwork is too heavy and too cumbersome for extensive use on stage.

Departing from conventional theatre practice, we find some problems of presentation that are partly solved by the scenic designer and partly by the architect. The famous Vieux Colombier theatre in Paris had a permanent set that was capable of many variations of level and entrance space. The architectural setting of the Festival Theatre at Stratford, Ontario, was designed by Tanya Moiseiwitsch. She has been associated with Sir Tyrone Guthrie for many years, and designed many of his productions. For this theatre, Guthrie wanted a setting that would serve, without alteration, for Shakespearian plays. The architectural setting at the Chichester Festival Theatre was designed by the architect, and it can be taken down to make way for structures specifically designed by scenic artists. The Maddermarket Theatre has a set designed to suggest the Elizabethan theatre, but, for modern plays, ordinary scenery is often set in front of the permanent structure. Further examples of architectural settings, such as those at the Mermaid Theatre and the Unicorn Theatre at Abingdon help us to form the conclusion that each is a highly individual proposition. And because scenery itself is not usually required there is no need to comment on them further.

A particular sort of permanent setting is, however, more common. This is the curtain set. A complete curtain setting can be used in the production of a play, without bringing in any scenery. A simple arras set, with side curtains, is extremely serviceable. But it is usual to bring in at any rate some scenery. This may be by the addition of a painted backcloth, or of doors, windows and fireplaces which are placed between curtains. There are many different and ingenious ways of putting the permanent and temporary pieces together. But I want to stress the value, in a small theatre, of a complete set of black curtains to serve as a mask for backstage spaces and as a neutral background to scenery. In front of this background you can set cut-down flats, screens and independent three-dimensional pieces such as platforms, rocks or trees. The scenery can be set very easily, and where it is not possible to fly and where wing space is restricted, very ambitious productions can be undertaken with great economy.

VI

PAINTING SCENERY

WHEN you are going to paint scenery you must have a room with plenty of space. The room will get dirty from top to bottom. The size and number of pieces to be painted at any one time will vary and it is impossible to say exactly how big the paint shop should be. Most paint shops, except the very biggest, will probably be concerned with scenery for a single theatre. It should therefore be large enough to set up all the flats required on the stage of the theatre for any single scene. That is to say, it should be at least the size of the acting area. The room should accommodate the largest cloth likely to be used, either by hanging it against a wall or spreading it flat on the floor. Doors and access to the room should be big enough to allow to pass the largest flats, cloths and solids that are likely to be used.

Painting Flats

The best way of painting flats for a box set is to stand them next to each other in the order in which they will be set up on the stage. This usually means leaning them against the four walls of the paint shop. The amateur designer will be very lucky if he has a paint frame, which is part of the equipment of many big theatres. It is a counterweighted wooden frame, big enough to take the largest cloth used in the theatre or a complete set of flats, and to it the scenery is temporarily nailed, in an upright position, while being painted. The frame can be lowered into a slot in the floor so that all painting may be done at floor level. In the absence of a frame it may be useful to have a special boomerang (a platform on wheels) with several levels. The top level should be high enough to let the painter reach the highest flats. Each level should be big enough to accommodate painter, buckets of paint and brushes. The boomerang is preferable to ladders—it is much safer and steadier.

However, many painters have no paint frames, boomerangs

68

or even space enough to stand a set of flats up against the walls. It is possible to paint flats one by one laid out on trestles in the middle of the room. They can be taken outside or into another room to dry. Measurements affecting horizontal lines, such as skirting board, picture rails and so on, and patterns have to be checked carefully as the first time you see the set put together may be on stage.

Paint-shop Equipment

No matter how small the room is, you must have a water tap, somewhere to pour away waste and to wash brushes, and you must have a good gas-ring or two for heating up buckets of paint. An electric ring will do, but it will probably not be quite so happy with the water and rough usage that it will receive. It is useful to have a trolley, perhaps an old domestic tea trolley, to serve as a portable palette. You will need a number of buckets for mixing paint in, a number of paint cans for carrying small quantities of paint, mixing sticks, and a large tin bath for mixing whitening in. A dry and substantial cupboard is desirable for storing paint powders and size. You will also need, sooner or later, a straight-edge, which should be made the full length of the flats up to ten feet or at any rate at least six feet long. The straight-edge should be constructed of two pieces of timber so that the edge itself is well clear of the canvas. It is sensible to mark the straight-edge in inches and feet. A chalk-line may be helpful, particularly when you are painting cloths. It is a piece of thin cord and is rubbed with chalk or charcoal, whichever will make the clearer mark on the canvas; the centre is lifted and allowed to snap down on to the canvas, leaving a straight line.

Brushes

There are different sorts of brushes for different jobs. You will need two or three distemper brushes between four inches and six inches wide. These will be for priming and painting a first colour in large areas. You should have a selection of paint brushes between half an inch and four inches to be used for more detailed work and for painting three-dimensional pieces. You will probably be using several colours at once and may need more brushes than you think, as you will not want

6—(G.383)

to keep washing out a brush every time you come to a different colour on each flat. You should have a selection of fitches, or small brushes, and a number of different sized lining fitches (which have bristles specially cut at an angle to help in making straight lines). It is worth buying expensive brushes. They last a long time and their hairs stay firm. They should be looked after carefully. This means, wash your brushes after use and hang them up, bristle downwards. It is a good idea to drill the handles so that brushes can easily be suspended from nails on the front of a shelf.

Paints

Paint for flats and cloths is a mixture of dry powdered distemper colour, with size and water. Size can be bought in powder form, or jellied. Paint sellers usually have a chart of colours to choose from. Colours vary in price, and utility. A basic supply might include—

Whitening	Venetian Red
Black	Dark Green
Yellow Ochre	Ultramarine Blue
Vandyke Brown	

Some colours, such as jade green and vermilion, are expensive to buy; some such as prussian blue and scarlet, are difficult to paint over with a different colour and should be avoided if the scenery goes into stock to be painted again; some paints can be bought already mixed with size but they are more expensive. Consult your supplier on these matters. Whitening is cheap, and used in large quantities.

The first ingredients of paint to prepare are size and water. Jellied size is put in a bucket on a gas-ring and left to melt. It is sensible to add a cupful of hot water. When using powdered size, heat a bucket of water and while it is boiling slowly stir in the size with a stick. Use about one pound of size to two gallons of water.

Mix a large quantity of whitening. It can be kept mixed in a tin bath ready for whenever you want it and you will probably need about as much as all other colours put together. It usually comes in lumps which should be crumbled up, by hand, until the bath is half filled or more. Pour in cold water until the whitening is covered and leave it to soak for twenty-four hours. It will need stirring before use as the water tends to rise clear to the top. If there are any lumps, they should be kneaded by hand. This solution, mixed with an equal quantity of size solution, makes a good priming paint.

Prepare pigment by half filling a bucket or can with the powder, using the required colour. Add water, stirring until you have a smooth, creamy paste, without lumps. If whitening is needed to give the desired colour mix it in now. Add to this an equal quantity of size solution; and stir well. The paint is now ready. It can be used hot or cold. Always mix plenty of each colour to be used as water paint nearly always dries a different shade from the original wet paint, and it is therefore extremely difficult to mix a good match. The final colour can be checked roughly while mixing if a piece of paper is given a brush stroke and then dried rapidly near the flame of the gas-ring. Until you have had a good deal of experience, it will dry paler than you think. Whitening solution is added to pigment solution, particularly of a pale colour, to give it body. This is particularly important when painting over a previous design of dark colours, which otherwise tend to show through. Size in solution goes stale and makes a smell that most people find unpleasant. If the solution is likely to be kept for more than a few days, two or three teaspoonfuls of carbolic acid may be mixed in the solution to stop it from decomposing.

Painting Techniques

New canvas should be given a priming coat of warm whitening and size solution or other paint. Yesterday's paints can be boxed together (poured back and forth from one container to another), warmed up and used for a priming coat. Using a four-inch or six-inch brush, spread the paint evenly, smoothly and not too thickly all over the canvas, including round the edges of flats. Allow this coat of paint to dry thoroughly. It may take up to six hours depending on the atmosphere and temperature in the paint shop. The same procedure is followed when applying a ground colour which goes over the prime coat or the previous design. It is usually necessary to paint over the ground colour to apply pattern or texturing, depending on the design of the set.

When flats have been primed, make the necessary lines to indicate main areas of ground colour and lay these in first, using four-inch or six-inch brushes. Don't forget to paint the edges of flats. This is likely to be a day's work. The next day the canvas will be ready for the next step—the application of pattern, texture or further colour.

Flats for an interior set usually require a number of horizontal lines to mark such things as skirting board, dado, picture rail, frieze, panelling or architraves round doors and windows. All measurements should be taken from the bottom of flats as even new flats may be slightly different in overall height. Lines, such as those making a picture rail, are painted in highlight and shadow. Using a charcoal stick, mark both sides of the flat and join the marks across the flat using a straight-edge or snap-line. An inch or so below your guide line, using a lining fitch, paint a dark line to represent the shadow below the curve. Before this line has completely dried, paint another line above it, lighter than the ground colour, to represent the highlight. These lines will merge slightly, giving a rounded effect. Take the lines round both side edges. This principle can be extended to more complicated mouldings, panels and so on, but care should be taken in measuring the height of lines so that adjacent flats match up.

Wallpaper patterns can be made with stencils. You can cut your own from stiff brown paper (or thin show card) which is then varnished on both sides with knotting. Or you can use templates. Stencils should be painted in with a short, stiffish brush and the paint applied as drily as possible, with only a little in the brush at each dip. A template, giving an outline shape, or half a shape, can be cut from hardboard and then followed on the canvas with charcoal or brush; the pattern is filled in as necessary. A delicate pattern can be marked by pricking out the pattern in stiff paper, using a pin or small nail. The stencil is held in position and the lines of holes are dabbed with a small cotton bag, containing finely powdered charcoal. With all patterns care must be taken that the flats are marked so that repeated designs fall where required.

Less formal patterns can be made by rolling with a sponge roller. It is easy to cut rough patterns in sponge rubber. You can use an ordinary paint roller or make your own with a

rolling pin. Or simply dab paint on, fairly dry, at regular
intervals, with a sponge that has acquired a certain rough
character of its own.

Interior walls whether patterned or not will almost certainly
be improved by the appearance of texture. With plain walls,
texture can be suggested when painting the first coat by having
two buckets with slightly different versions of the basic colour
and dipping the brush alternately into each bucket. Or, after
painting the basic colour and before it is quite dry, lightly
make strokes with a dry brush in different directions all over
it—using the variant colour. These techniques impart a rough
finish—which is, incidentally, useful as a start for stone or
brickwork, with appropriate colours. Sponging and rolling
can be applied for the same purpose. Dry brushing can be
used to simulate wood grain. Interesting textures can be
obtained by spattering. When the groundwork is quite dry,
dip a four-inch brush generously into paint of a quite different
colour and, with a snap of the wrist, throw spray on to the
canvas. It is more restful to the wrists, but noisier, to hold a
twelve-inch piece of 3-in. × 1-in., or other timber, in one hand
and knock the brush against it again and again with the other.
Spatter generously, and by all means with more than one
colour, but avoid too wet a spray which will dribble down the
canvas. Though this might give an effect you will want one
day!

These painting techniques can also be used to give light and
shade. Even in the most ordinary room no two walls reflect the
same amount of light and even one wall will show variations of
light intensity. These variations are usually quite noticeable in
the corners of a room. Besides, the designer may want to shade
the walls in order to concentrate attention, perhaps, at the
bottom of the set rather than let eyes wander too much to
frieze level. Certainly nothing looks more artificial and unnatural than a set of flats covered with real wallpaper, plain
and simple. It does not achieve the effect desired but, as a rule,
draws attention to what is usually in such cases the blatant
absurdity of stage lighting; compartment battens are probably
used and they spread an unnatural glare over the entire surface.
Shadow and texturing would help. Better still, paint the whole
thing.

Most of the suggestions that I have made so far apply to interior and ordinary scenes, made up of flats. When you are painting a cloth or an irregular design, direct measurements cannot be used for a start. A complex shape is transferred from the design to canvas by the process of squaring off. A piece of tracing paper, on which has been ruled, in the scale of the design, a grid to give one-foot or two-foot squares, is placed securely over the design. The canvas is similarly divided with lines made with the straight-edge or snap-line. The outlines of design can now be copied square by square with charcoal. Any charcoal lines that show when painting has been finished can be rubbed out with a duster.

Three-dimensional pieces, such as doors, windows and fireplaces are usually painted with scene paint, but I prefer to use emulsion paint. It is a water paint and can be used in much the same way as scene paint. It has the advantage of being ready for use, it dries quickly, it will stand up to a good deal of handling, it can be cleaned simply with a damp cloth, and it can easily be touched up. Emulsion paint is expensive, but large quantities will not be required. Most firms show on their colour cards a range of pastel shades. But stronger colours can be obtained, and I have enjoyed using many of the House and Garden colours in Interlight emulsion paint made by International Paints. When using emulsion paint, it is particularly important to clean brushes thoroughly, immediately after use, using plenty of cold water. Emulsion paint is particularly suitable for props, furniture and solid scenery. Incidentally, don't use ordinary paints with an oil base as they take a long time to dry, and usually have a gloss which may reflect light in unexpected ways on the stage.

I can think of no other rules for painting solid scenery. The ideas already put forward may be helpful. The designer must invent his own techniques if necessary. Sometimes materials will be used that require no paint—Perspex, expanded metal or Fibreglass perhaps. Sometimes conventional scene paint may be used on timber or hardboard—dry brush, spattering and all. But care should be taken that the paint adheres adequately and does not rub off or come away in the course of ordinary usage.

VII

SETTING UP AND LIGHTING

CANVAS flats are light and easy to use but they can be damaged if they are wrongly handled, and paintwork can be spoiled by carelessness. Let us start with the simplest jobs and go on to describe a complete set-up.

Handling and Setting up Flats

To raise a flat lying on the floor, take hold of the centre of one stile and lift the flat so that it rests vertically on the other. Keep your hands off the paintwork and on the back of the framework, as far as possible. Holding the flat in this position, go to the bottom of the flat and, putting a foot against the lower corner, use both hands to grip the upper corner and give it a sharp pull. When it comes up to its vertical position you can hold the flat by the stile. To run the flat, stand sideways to it, facing the direction you are going to move and grasp the leading edge with your near hand raised high and the other hand, arm across your body, at waist level; keep the flat leaning slightly towards you and raise the leading edge, and you can then run the flat to any place on the stage. Rapid movement helps keep the flat in balance. A flat can easily be lowered to the floor by floating; that is, having made sure the floor is quite clear and clean, you put you foot against the centre of the bottom rail and let the flat fall away from you. The air will cushion its descent.

Scenery should be stacked for storage as nearly vertical as possible, and it is usually good practice to have painted surfaces face to face. Identification is helped by painting the name of the play, the scene and a code number to indicate position on the back of each flat.

The method of setting up flats on stage will depend on the changes or performance of the setting, the production schedule and the technical facilities available. There may be a grid system so that scenery can be flown out, or trucks so that scenery can be rolled away, or elevators to take scenery below

75

FIG. 33 (a)–(d). LIFTING A FLAT

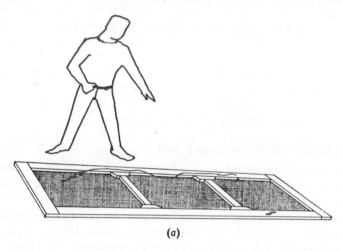

(a)

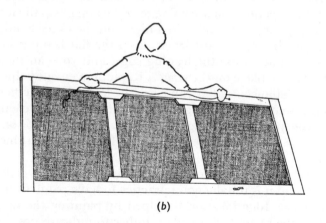

(b)

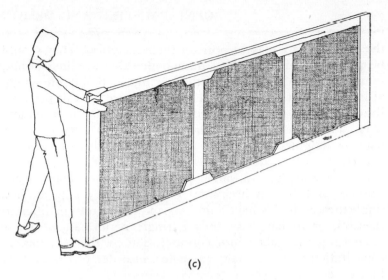

(c)

(d)

the stage. There may be none of these facilities. They should be used if they are available. But whether they are there or not, some if not all of the scenery can be set up by the simple system of lashing. Flats are provided with furniture for this purpose. Braces may be used for added strength and for independent flats. These are screwed to the floor, if it is a softwood stage floor, or weighted. Some flats are fitted with their own french braces.

A play may have a single permanent set or many scene changes, and the play itself may settle down for a long run in a single theatre, it may have a limited run, it may tour in different theatres, or it may have only a single performance. These factors must be taken into consideration by the designer, in consultation with the stage manager, in order to decide how best to set up.

A permanent set, or a set on a revolve or truck stage that is going to be used for a long run, must be fixed as securely as possible. It is quite sensible to screw or nail the flats together, making a permanent join. But if the setting has to be struck many times, or even if the flats have to be used again, continuous nailing and pulling apart is likely to cause unnecessary damage.

The commonest way of setting up is to make use of lashlines and braces. This method works adequately under most circumstances, and does no harm to the flats. It is ideal for the permanent setting made up of stock flats that must be used again, and it allows scene changes to be made fairly quickly by a skilled crew. Inexperienced stage hands may make a lot of noise with lashlines and be very slow moving flats. But great speed can be achieved and the change effected in very near silence. Finally, a grid is a great aid to rapid and silent scene changing provided it is high enough to enable scenery to be flown out.

When lashing flats together, work from behind them. With two flats aligned in position, hold them together in place with the left hand. Take the lashline in your right hand, steady it and then make a quick circular movement upwards and to the side so as to make a loop run up the line. Guide the line so that the loop engages the top cleat of the other flat and pull taut again. If there are intermediate cleats, engage these in a similar fashion until you reach the tie-off cleats. Take the line under both these cleats then round the standing part above the cleats and pull smartly down on the loop thus formed. Tie off with a bow hitch, which should be quite secure. It can easily be undone, when the time comes, with a tug at the loose end.

Flats may have to be joined edge to edge or on an inside corner or an outside corner. Butt joins should if possible run parallel to the proscenium line so that the joint cannot easily be seen by the audience. Stop cleats fitted to flats that have to be joined edge to edge or on outside corners help in getting a good join, and blocks can be fitted on a flat to help an inside join. A setting designed with a number of angles will usually be quite rigid as soon as the flats are lashed together. But extra security may be required for door flats. This is provided by braces. These are also used for independent flats such as backings and groundrows, and to give security to runs of several flats in line.

Stage braces are usually made in two pieces so that the length can be adjusted. One end is hooked so that it can engage a screw eye fitted to the flat, and the other end has a foot iron designed to take a stage screw or a stage weight. The stage screw gives the better support, but it cannot be used on a floor made, for instance, of polished hardwood, and weights must be resorted to. A stage weight is effective on a polished floor if the brace is first screwed to a wooden base that has a rubber pad glued to its under surface.

Ground rows, and scenic units that are not liable to be moved out of place by accident, are best supported by french braces which are simply hinged to the back of the flat. French braces may be weighted with sandbags for security.

Scenery that has been set up as described will be secure. And it can be easily shifted by undoing braces, unlashing the flats one by one, and running them away. Well-organized stacks of flats, and special places for braces and weights in the wings help to achieve a reasonably quick scene change. In many theatres this is the only way of shifting scenery. But where a grid is fitted, it provides the quickest and quietest way of changing scene, and, since spare scenery is flown out, it keeps the stage floor clear.

Flying Scenery

A grid may make use of the Renaissance system of ropeline rigging that depends on strength of arm or it may employ the more modern system of counterweighted lines. Uncommon, but more efficient, are multiple-speed counterweight systems, and the new synchronous, electronically controlled winches. The latter is an American speciality devised by George Izenour. It it not likely to be met in this country.

Scenery that is to be flown should be fitted with the appropriate hanging irons. These must be bolted on; screws are not good enough. Heavy flats or runs of flats should have hanger irons on the bottom rails and hooks on the top rails so that lines can be attached to the bottom of the unit, taking the weight and keeping joints under compression, while the top hooks engage round the lines and hold the flats upright. This is also the best way of rigging units that must be unfastened when set. When a counterweight system is used, sandbags must be ready for snapping on to lines before scenery is freed.

The procedure for flying scenery must be followed carefully. Your stage plan will show you the appropriate set of lines for each unit. Lower the batten nearly to the floor. Lock the lines. Lay the scenery face down with the upper rails immediately under the batten. Fasten the hanging irons to the batten, with wire or chain lengths. Put the necessary counterweights in the cradle, release the lines and raise the scenery to vertical position. Finally make any necessary adjustments to ensure good balance and proper trim. When the production is over and the scenery has to be removed, reverse the procedure.

Rolling Units

Whether or not the stage is equipped with wagons you will find that rolling units are extremely useful. The rigid platform already described can easily be fitted with castors, and serves the purpose admirably. The castors should be able to swivel and be fitted with rubber tyres. They must be carefully chosen for the weight they are to carry. The rolling platform, or boat truck as it is called, can be held in position on stage by wedges introduced between the floor and the undersides of the platform on opposite sides. A boat truck of this sort can be used to shift solid units and heavy pieces of scenery that are too bulky to fly.

With ingenuity, a boat truck can be two-faced and serve the purpose of a small revolving stage. More complicated wagons may be self-powered by battery-driven electric motors. Four of these were among the devices called for by Sean Kenny in his designs for *Blitz*.

Routine for Setting Up

All sorts of factors must be considered when scheduling the routine for setting up, and the following description can only be a rough guide. It would be too confusing to try and reckon with all possible circumstances. As a preliminary with the aid of the ground plan, mark in with chalk a few key points of the setting on the stage floor.

Scenery that is to be flown is rigged first (including special lighting equipment) and it is then flown out if necessary. Now free standing three-dimensional pieces are moved into position. Next all flats are lashed together in place, starting, if possible, downstage, on the O.P. side and working round the set in order. Sometimes it is preferable to start setting from the centre line. Three-dimensional units that attach to flats, such as doors and windows, are now fixed in place. Finally backings are positioned, ceiling or borders let in and groundrows and borders brought in.

Sightlines must be checked, then the position of each flat should be marked on the floor with paint, and the flats themselves marked for identification. Lashing and braces should be checked, doors tested and adjustments made as necessary. The set can now be furnished, dressed and lit and then, if appropriate, struck and stacked.

To cope with a number of scene changes in a single play, it is not always necessary to strike completely and reset. Machinery, such as the revolve or wagon stage, is intended to save the trouble, but it is not usually available in small theatres. The designer may plan the settings so that one can be set up permanently and another be fitted inside it. This is particularly appropriate when the play calls for one main and one subsidiary set. It can be managed very easily if there is a grid and the inner set is flown. The designer can cope with scene changes by having a false proscenium with small changeable pieces, particularly appropriate for revue; by having a semi-permanent

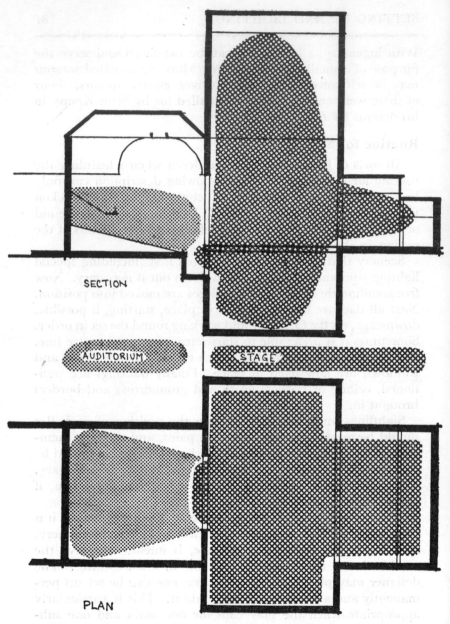

SECTION

AUDITORIUM   STAGE

PLAN

FIG. 35. PLAN AND SECTION OF A CONVENTIONAL PROSCENIUM THEATRE,
INDICATING PROPORTIONS BETWEEN AUDITORIUM SPACE AND MAIN STAGE
SPACE

Front-of-house facilities, such as foyer and refreshment space,
have not been included

setting with some changeable units. It is also possible to make use of a special spotlight or projector to provide different backgrounds. A projector can be used in other ways as well and is likely to be of importance for open-stage work where the floor of the acting area can be patterned with light. But we are now getting into highly specialized fields and these can be left for the specialist to explore.

The Lighting Designer

In the big theatres of London and New York, a new expert is making his way into the production team, the lighting designer. As his name implies, he is a designer in a very real sense and he specializes in light rather than in scenery. But the effect of scenery depends a good deal on lighting, and the two designers should work hand in hand. In small theatres lighting is more often arranged by the producer, but frequently the designer is consulted and he sometimes takes charge alto-gether. Whether he takes charge of the lighting or not, he should learn all he can about it. It will be useful, perhaps to remind you of basic principles. For a start, there are three aspects of lighting that can be swiftly summarized.

Principles of Lighting

Ever since it has become possible to control artificial sources of light the main purpose of stage lighting has been to illuminate the actors and the stage, thus helping to focus the attention of the audience on the acting area. What is not lit cannot be seen. Artificial light usually comes from a relatively small source, a lamp, and a number of these lamps are used. The simplest way to enable an audience to see an actor would be to shine lamps as near as possible along the lines of sight. There are two reasons for not doing this. Firstly, it would be difficult to arrange positions for placing the lamps. They would have to be pretty well mixed up with the audience's heads. Secondly, light along the lines of sight would tend to flatten out the three-dimensional characteristics of the actor's face and form—there would be no shadows or differences of intensity by which the audience could discern three-dimensional shapes. In order to see the form of actors—and objects on the

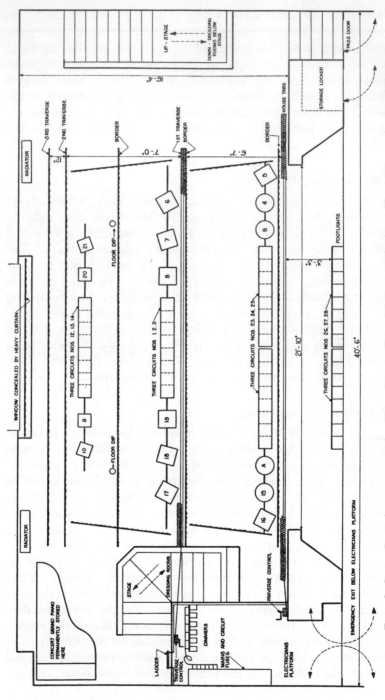

FIG. 36. STAGE PLAN (PREPARED BY THE HULL GARRET PLAYERS) OF THE FARMERY HALL, KINGSTON UPON HULL

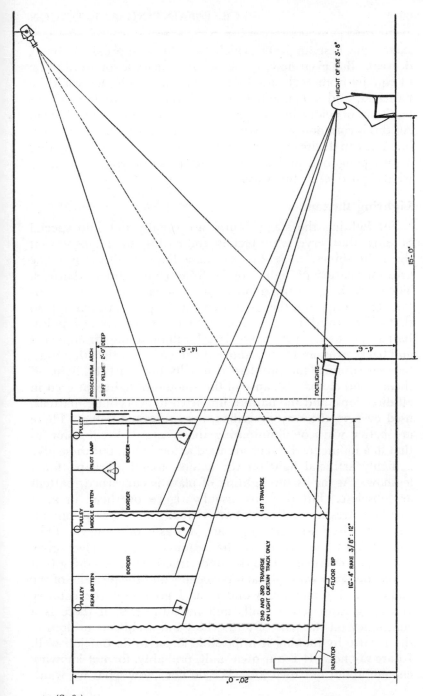

FIG. 37. SECTION OF THE STAGE OF THE FARMERY HALL, KINGSTON UPON HULL

stage—the best angle at which to light is approximately 45 degrees. But even now, if a centrally placed actor were to be lit equally from each side by lamps at this angle, he would be flattened, and it is useful to use differences of angle or of intensity or of colour in order to preserve three-dimensional form. All this is common sense, with some elementary physics thrown in. You can devise experiments with a couple of torches lighting a ping-pong ball and a small cube to show yourself exactly what light does in this way.

Lighting Battens

For lighting the stage, lamps are usually put into special housings that serve as protection and enclose the lamps so that the light shines, more or less, in a limited direction. The greatest scatter of light comes from compartment battens. These are long strips, divided into compartments each containing a lamp, and they are often wired up in three circuits so that every third lamp is linked to the same control point. Battens are used on the stage floor for illuminating groundrows and backcloths, and flown above the stage for borders that must be seen (though the problem is usually how to keep light off them!) and cloths. Because of the amount of light scattered in all directions, and the flatness imparted to everything, battens, used even in the way described, are of limited value. There are better ways of illuminating the scenery. We'll come to that in a moment. Battens are used as footlights, but these give a highly artificial light on the actors—useful, perhaps, for a legshow. As far as the lighting of plays is concerned, battens are obsolete. But they are usually rigged overhead in most small theatres and halls that have virtually no other equipment. In these circumstances they are a waste of money. They cannot light the actors at the required angle. They give, instead, an overhead glare that is destructive of everything that a good designer wants for actors, scenery and the pleasure of the audience. I sometimes wonder, as I go round the country visiting various school halls and little theatres, if there is a conspiracy on the part of authorities and architects to destroy the theatre by making it impossible for us to do our job well. I dare say not. It is our own fault, probably, for not knowing enough about our own job. We do not know what we want,

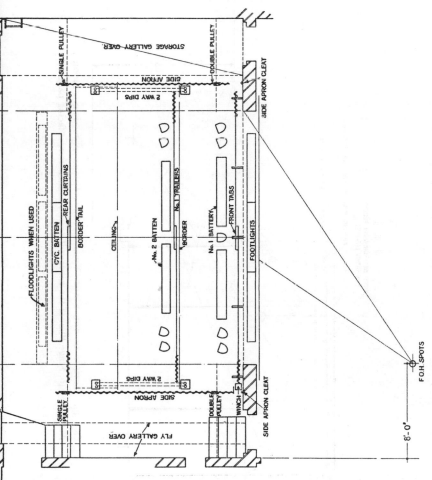

FIG. 38. STAGE PLAN, MADE BY WATTS AND CORRY, OF THE VILLAGE HALL,
HOLME-ON-SPALDING-MOOR

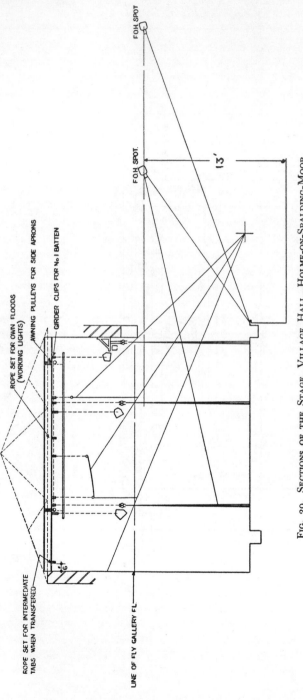

FOH SPOT

FOH SPOT.

13'

ROPE SET FOR OWN FLOODS
(WORKING LIGHTS)

AWNING PULLEYS FOR SIDE APRONS

GIRDER CLIPS FOR No.1 BATTEN

ROPE SET FOR INTERMEDIATE
TABS WHEN TRANSFERED

LINE OF FLY GALLERY FL

Fig. 39. Sections of the Stage, Village Hall, Holme-on-Spalding-Moor
(*Note.* Fig. 40, Stage Plan of the Library Theatre, Manchester, is facing page 90)

we do not know how to use the equipment we have, we do not take enough interest in technical and artistic developments. We have all these awful battens, let us admit it, because these are what we have asked for. But there is a growing recognition of the need for directional light. So let us now take a good look at instruments and their uses.

Floodlights and Spotlights

The lamp in a compartment batten will probably have a wattage of 60, 100 or 150 watts—a familiar domestic lamp in fact. A more powerful lamp, enclosed in its own casing, serves as a floodlight. The light spreads out over a wide angle. The casing is designed so that the floodlight can be mounted on a stand. The main use of the floodlight is for illuminating cloths and scenic pieces from the side—the stands being in the wings. Many floodlights are made so that hoods can be put over them, reducing the angle of spread, and they can thus be used to contribute to the main lighting. The main lighting, however, must be more restricted in spread and optical apparatus is necessary—lenses, reflectors and so on. The instruments that have been devised to give the main lighting for the stage are spotlights. They are comparatively expensive. If looked after, they are efficient. It is worth knowing enough about your own spotlights to enable you to get the best out of them. But since each manufacturer produces many different instruments, all I can do is to recommend that you take note of the technical information that is readily available from your dealers. The beam of light from a spotlight may have a hard edge (a profile spot, as it is called), which is particularly useful for front-of-house lighting, as diaphragms can be placed in the light to restrict the beam within the proscenium—there is no need to spill light all over the proscenium arch unless you want to. Another kind of spotlight, the soft edge spotlight, is more useful on stage, and the beam mixes easily with the beams from other lights, without sharp changes of light on the actors as they move across the stage. Sometimes a spotlight, such as the Strand Electric pattern 23 baby spot, is primarily a profile spot, but a change of lens or the addition of a diffusing glass will turn it into a soft edge spotlight. The Strand Electric pattern 123 Fresnel spotlight is designed as a soft edge spotlight and is ideal. Nearly all spotlights can be focused down to a narrow angle or opened up to a fairly wide angle; this is done by a control at the bottom of the casing, or by moving the lens assembly, or by a screw control at the back of the casing. Profile spotlights may have various diaphragms for adjusting the size and shape of the beam. Ordinary soft edge spotlights may be fitted with hoods for restricting spill. All spotlights can be provided with frames for holding colour media. Some spotlights can be adjusted to project transparencies, but this is usually an expensive business and is sufficiently specialized for me to leave it to the expert.

The major part of lighting for the stage should come from spotlights, and these should be mounted so that their beams reach the acting area at an angle of about 45 degrees from the horizontal. I am omitting any reference here to special effects. This means that, in most theatres and halls where a proscenium has been provided, much of the lighting should be positioned in the auditorium. It is called front-of-house lighting. This is particularly important if there is an apron or forestage. It must be distributed so that it can come from either side— though some can come from the centre of the auditorium as well. Further, if spotlights are to be used to advantage they must be easily accessible. In an ordinary hall, front-of-house lighting is often mounted on brackets on the walls, where a ladder can be placed. This is satisfactory. A more elaborate idea, and a preferable one, is to have special openings in the ceiling that can be got at from above by catwalks in the roof. However simple or elaborate the system of mounting front-of-house lighting, it is the key to good work on the proscenium stage. It must give light at the correct angle and be accessible. Incidentally, lighting the open stage or theatre in the round presents no special problems. Spotlights are the main lighting instruments and their beams should reach the acting area at approximately 45 degrees. I favour the Strand pattern 123 already referred to. I don't know why it is that so many people coming freshly to the idea of open staging imagine that lighting must come from directly overhead, as though you were lighting a billiard table—and turning actors heads into billiard balls! The only additional requirement for theatre in the round is that spotlights must be grouped on all sides of the acting area, and for the three-sided stage lighting must embrace at least as much of the acting area as the audience does.

I wonder if I have put enough emphasis on the fact that most lighting should come from spotlights and at an angle of about 45 degrees from the horizontal? There it is again just in case! I had better add—abolish battens. They will probably be the the main equipment in most small theatres so be prepared to replace them with spotlights. And if, as is likely to be the case, the designer finds that there is not enough light coming from the best positions, he must do what he can to put matters right. But though it is justifiable to underline this matter, it is wrong to be too dogmatic. In addition to the main lighting, other light can come from all sorts of angles, and some special effects will depend on beams shooting from the oddest of angles—it is up to you to choose what you want to do. A stage is usually equipped with socket outlets in the wings, often dips let into the floor, and usually there are special brackets just inside the proscenium wall for perch spots, and sometimes facilities for rigging booms (vertical bars) that carry spotlights on brackets. There is nearly always a horizontal bar just inside the proscenium arch, the number 1 bar, for carrying the main on-stage lighting. The distribution of spotlights, together with subsidiary lighting from floods can determine the overall appearance of the stage, the appearance of the actors and the setting. Each lighting instrument is individually wired to a distribution board where control of brightness is possible. Much depends on the number of dimmers available. A good lighting board will enable every circuit to be separately controlled by dimmer, but one is not always provided. The designer should make sure exactly what can be done with the lighting board. He will have to rely on it.

Use of Light and Colour

Finally, let me go back to the matter of colour. I mentioned that colour can be used to help give form to solid objects, and for this purpose the subtlest and palest of colours can be used as long as there is contrast from different sides. Some people prefer to use strong colour. Sir Tyrone Guthrie has developed a system of stage lighting that does without colour entirely. I

like to use colour rarely, if only because it cuts out a considerable amount of sheer light. But when I do use colours, I like
them strong. Some producers use certain colours for special
effects—blue for moonlight (though moonlight is not blue and
the blue that many producers use is enough to put you off
colour altogether), red for firelight (though firelight is not red,
alas!). Some people are sensitive to the emotional power of
colour, though I am not one of them. But I have a penchant
for peacock blue in eerie scenes and orange in scenes of the
hotter emotions. The way you use colour will depend on your
taste and talent—and I strongly recommend that you use it
sparingly until you are sure that you have established your
good taste and have developed a real talent.

I am not going to say anything in general about the way to
light the stage. It would take far too long to give a fair description of any particular system, of which there are several, and
each production requires fresh treatment. There are plenty of
good books on the subject to help the beginner. But there is
something that I feel very strongly about lighting, and, indeed,
about all technical matters connected with the theatre.
Lighting (and all technical equipment) is supposed to help the
actor in his performance to the audience, and it should not
draw attention away from the actors—either by being particularly clever or particularly bad. If you cannot manage
technical matters properly, leave them alone. Illuminate the
stage because you must, but don't suppose it is necessary to
take the lights up and down—unless it is helpful to the actors
and the play and you have the technical efficiency to do it
properly. One learns the hard way. I produced a number of
plays in a Women's Institute Hall that had no dimmer board.
We switched the lights on at the beginning of the play, and
they stayed on until the end. But I was not content. I borrowed
a switchboard from a friend who was manager of a big theatre
that had just been re-equipped. It arrived just before the dress
rehearsal of *An Inspector Calls* and I fell into the temptation of
arranging a complicated lighting schedule to give the production a cinematic effect. There were seventy-nine lighting
cues. The stage manager didn't miss one; but they were not
very well conceived as you may guess. After the first night I
listened in the foyer for comment—and sure enough two old

ladies were discussing the production. One said "Did you notice the lights going up and down, dear?" and her friend replied, "Yes, there must have been a power failure." But it is wrong to sit back and avoid all technical matters. Lighting is one of the most powerful aids that an actor has, and the designer or producer, whoever is responsible, must be technically proficient and learn to light each play properly.

VIII

THE DESIGNING PROCESS

I DO not believe that there is any important sense in which the designing of scenery differs from the designing of any-thing else. A knowledge of materials, a sympathy with techniques, a love of work, and a sense of purpose are always more or less the distinguishing features of a good designer. There is little point, I think, in making a special study of form and colour in relation to scenery. Form and colour should be studied as fundamentals that will affect all design, and they are best dealt with in a course of basic design. Further, although I have dealt with materials to some extent, there are huge potential developments to be made with new materials, and familiar materials can be used in highly unorthodox ways to good effect. But having already described, though briefly, the various isolated elements in the scene designer's craft, it might be useful if I now try and show how a designer actually gets to work on the isolated business of designing. It must be necessarily a highly personal affair, and, in the main, what follows is nothing more than some notes about a few of my own designs. I shall, in spite of myself, disclose some irrelevant prejudices which you will probably recognize easily enough, and, from the start, my choice of play may be unusual and arbitrary. But not, I hope, uninteresting!

The Sets for "The Lunatic View"

The Lunatic View is the sort of play that is likely to appeal to a small company, specializing in modern and unusual produc-tions. The play has not been presented in the West End, but the author, David Campton, is fairly well-known for his off-beat sense of humour, original ideas and carefully composed dialogue. The play is published in an edition that is unusually free of stage directions. The reason for this will become clear in a moment. I gave the play its first production and prepared it for publication, and I can confirm that this is what both author and producer wanted. The play turns out to be of

94

unusual shape. It is not a straightforward full-length play, but a series of short plays, four in number, which the author calls "glimpses." Each play is introduced by a radio announcer, but only the first actually involves the radio itself. When you have read the plays, you will probably agree that each of them gives a quick picture of some aspect of modern society. The thing they have in common is the author's attitude to his material. All the characters seem to be living in a perilous world, and they are unaware of their situation. You want to shout out to them: "Look out!" But they go blindly on their way— in most cases to destruction. The situations and the ways the characters behave are comical. The author calls the play a comedy of menace. We laugh at the characters. But he clearly intends the ideas to last longer than the laughter, and the result is both highly entertaining and deeply disturbing. These general considerations are of importance in preparing settings for a production. Let us go on to examine each play separately to see what the practical requirements are.

"A Smell of Burning" shows Mrs. and Mr. Jones at the breakfast table. The author gives us no further description of the setting. But we soon gather that the Joneses live in respectable middle-class surroundings, probably a flat (since they have a neighbour above), in a largish industrial town. They are visited by Mr. Robinson, Deputy Head of the City Surveyor's Department. There are no other characters. The Joneses have breakfast, and a toaster is an important property. The radio is on at the beginning of the play. Reference is made to the kitchen, a window is implied, the breakfast table is moved a few feet during the action, and there are, in this play as in two of the others, various sound effects.

"Memento Mori" contains only two characters, and takes place in a room in an empty house. Reference is made to a window, there is a large fireplace and two large cupboards with trick sliding doors—and in one of these cupboards the young man is shut, at the end of the play, to meet his macabre death. The floor-boards are solid, but reference to the rest of the house is vague. It seems to be an old house, and it is miles away from anywhere. The requirements are clear and simple, though there is a technical trick to be done with the sliding doors.

"Getting and Spending" is more complex. The author's directions say "The setting consists of two boxes—*his* and *hers* —and two doors—*inside* and *outside*." There are four characters in the piece, which introduces the newly-married Evelyn and Bobby and follows them through to old age. Meanwhile, the house that held such promise for them falls into ruins around them. This is something of challenge to the designer, particularly as the setting remains very much a background for the ageing and dilapidating characters.

"Then . . ." takes place in Piccadilly Circus, ruined by the bomb. There are only two characters, the last two in the world. And it is night-time, with moonlight.

To deal with these four plays in such a way as to get a coherent style, swift changes of setting and a reflection of the author's main intention, is our problem. Let us suppose two different productions, firstly in a small conventional theatre, and then with a small experimental group doing theatre in the round. The play has been presented at several small theatres, and by my own theatre in the round company, so the two productions have a basis in reality even though I have not, myself, built the settings for an actual production on an enclosed stage.

Firstly, then, let us prepare sketches for a production that will take place on a small stage. The proscenium opening is 24 ft, there are only 6 ft of wing space on each side, a depth of 16 ft, and no overhead flying space. Obviously it would be unwise to consider four complete box sets, and, luckily enough, such a treatment would not be appropriate to the play. Having accepted what may appear to be a limitation, you can now let the imagination expand. Let us consider first the name of the play and its division into "glimpses"; it becomes clear that the author is concerned with the visual aspects of presentation; the plays themselves confirm this—the dialogue reads well enough, but it demands action. Add the announcer. The idea begins to come forward, that the play might be staged behind a false proscenium in the shape of a television screen. There are never more than four actors on stage at any one moment, and usually only two, so the loss of acting-area space can be accepted. The whole of the décor could be carried out in black and white. This might help in getting a homogeneous effect for all the

glimpses. Further, if the lighting permits, it would be interesting to fill the false proscenium with a gauze that could be
painted with horizontal lines, suggesting television reception.
Each of the glimpses could have its own background in the
form of a small cut-out or book-flat. These would be set in a
surround of black curtains. When the gauze is lit from the
front-of-house spots it will be opaque, but as these lights are
dimmed and the on-stage lighting brought up, the gauze will
gradually disappear. It might be possible both to get a well-
defined view of the actors and to blur the edges of the gauze,
establishing a sort of barrier between actors and audience—
though this is something for the producer to decide. What sort
of cut-outs and book-flats? The first play could do with a
simple book, including a doorway (the door itself does not
seem necessary). This could be painted to suggest a wallpaper,
and the flats might benefit from an uneven profile, or fading
into blackness at the edges. The second play needs something
more complicated in the way of sliding doors. These could be
built solid, with the fireplace between them, and set behind
black tabs. The third play seems to need two doorways only.
The final play could be done with the help of a few blocks to
represent fallen masonry—the rest is darkness. Supposing the
producer agrees to a scheme of this sort for the production, we
can now proceed with sketches, ground-plan and detailed
drawings.

It is important to check that the scheme will fit into the
theatre and that where equipment, such as curtains and stage
lighting, is installed, it can be adapted for our use. I have
presumed a set of black surrounding curtains. If the theatre
already had grey surrounding curtains it might be a pity to put
them aside and hire blacks. They could be used. But a set of
brown curtains would mean sacrificing our idea of designing
the whole décor in black and white, and it might then be
justifiable to consider hiring black curtains from the start. The
precise nature and position of legs or wing pieces in a particular
theatre may suggest a modification to our intentions that would
not, in the end, make any real difference. But I have taken a
particular theatre, and will accordingly design for it.

The false proscenium is designed to suggest the shape of a
television screen. A television screen is usually nearly square.

It will be helpful if we remove any teaser and perhaps reduce the width of the opening. The frame will have to be specially constructed as this theatre's stock of flats includes nothing more than ten feet high. We can plan for three flats, two of them 17 ft × 4 ft and a header 20 ft × 2 ft. These flats will be profiled with hardboard, and a profile groundrow will complete

FIG. 41. SKETCH OF FALSE PROSCENIUM AND PERMANENT GAUZE
FOR *The Lunatic View* BY DAVID CAMPTON

the frame. The header will get support from the overhead bar that usually carries the teaser. The frame must be solidly fixed in place and the groundrow pieces will be screwed to the floor with angle brackets. A gauze will be stretched within the opening, and can be tacked back to the stiles of the flats. All that is wanted now is to paint the flats to look like a well finished TV set, in walnut perhaps—there is no need to estab-lish black, white and grey until we are behind the gauze.

Second thoughts on this false proscenium include the addi-tion of thickness to the supposed cabinet of the TV set. This could easily be provided by a six-inch strip of hardboard fixed to the profile pieces by corner blocks. It would mean that the

gauze would probably have to hang independently, but this is
no great difficulty provided we can suspend it immediately
upstage of the false proscenium, and provided the number 1 bar
allows enough downstage space for this. The theatre has no
apron stage, and we want to leave as little space below the
gauze as possible since a forestage cannot be made available to
the actors—without destroying the idea of a TV set. The
wastage of downstage space is going to be a difficulty, particularly when we come to consider the setting for the second play,
which must have a piece that will occupy the back three feet or
so of the stage, throughout the performance. It will be helpful,
then, to take another drastic decision, and abandon the main
curtain. The false proscenium can then be set hard against the
proscenium wall. This also ensures that we clear number 1 bar,
and gives more point to the gauze, which will conceal the acting
area until the play begins. Further, it might be a good idea to
write the name of the entertainment, *The Lunatic View*, on the
gauze or, more ambitiously, project on to it from the back of
the auditorium, and have slides made as titles for each of the
separate plays. This will increase the impression of a TV
screen. But if your theatre has a fire curtain, the Fire Officer
may not permit such a setting unless it is made of specially
fire-resistant materials.

The first setting consists of a book-flat, that is to say, two
flats hinged together so that, when open, they are self-support-
ing. One of these flats should contain a doorway. But a self-
supporting book-flat would not be firm enough to carry a door
unless it were braced. Even then, the door would be a source of
anxiety. In fact, the door is of no great importance in the play.
A hint is all that is wanted. And a doorway is perfectly adequate, though I should want to provide a thickness piece. The
flats will be set on the centre line, opened to form a right-angle,
the traverse curtains will come in to meet the edges of the flats,
otherwise the many entrances and exits of Mr. Robinson will be
difficult to effect—particularly the sudden appearance on cue
to say "Your hatchet," and the swift exit after "Boys—
playing." A table and two chairs will be set centrally, fairly
downstage. On one side of the room, a small table with a
radio on it, on the other side an imaginary window indicated
by a soft-edged spotlight shining from the wings.

The flats used can be taken from stock, and will be two
10-ft × 5-ft. In painting them I think a good modern wallpaper should be suggested. I wouldn't bother with a skirting
board since the scenic treatment is obviously sketchy, but I
should be tempted to consider the top of the flat as picture rail
level (though without actually painting the picture rail) and
sketch in a picture hanging on the wall. A picture of the Queen,

FIG. 42. SKETCH OF SETTING FOR "A Smell of Burning" IN DAVID
CAMPTON'S *The Lunatic View*

if the producer agrees to this, though the effect may be too
small to be useful to the audience.

The second play demands some mechanical ingenuity. There
have to be good, solid, sliding doors, and a good, solid fireplace.
I like to treat problems together—in fact I usually find, in
designing a set, that the solution to any single problem solves
several other problems as well, and if it doesn't I am always a
bit wary! A setting should be organic, and the right design
solves all problems. It fits the play, the stage, the lighting, the
actors and the budget. So an isolated problem is probably
something to promote rethinking along broad lines. But to
return to our doors. I propose to set a good solid unit incorporating the fireplace with a cupboard on each side of it,
against the back wall of the stage, and just above the back

curtains. This gives me about three feet of space. It is all that
is needed. The unit will consist of a framework, made from
Dexion slotted angle, on which can be mounted two four-foot
door flats from stock, and a header for over the fireplace.
Thickness pieces will be required inside the fireplace, and two
two-foot flats will serve the purpose. The doors will be made
of backing flats, equipped with wheels to run in a track on the
floor (Dexion will provide a guide at the top of the unit) for
the doors to slide in. When required, the doors can be manu-
ally operated by a stage-hand. For the second play, then, the
back curtains will be opened. The door into the room can be
imagined at one side, and the window, I think, might be effectively implied in the fourth wall—this will be very useful to the
actors at those moments when they are looking out into the
garden, "I thought of the garden too. In those days the beds
were properly made." The painting of the flats making up the
back unit should suggest fairly elaborate panelling. But it is
important that the whole set is fairly dark and gloomy. The
back wall of the stage serves as backing to the fireplace and the
cupboards. Behind the fireplace the wall might be given some
texture by dry brushing with black and grey paint. It might be
helpful to have the wall behind the cupboards brushed with
grey and white.

The author asks that the cupboard should extend from ceiling
to floor. "The men are dwarfed by the yawning black crack."
Our modest door flats may not be quite the right thing! It
might be better to use full-size flats for the sliding doors, with
full-size flats, 10 ft × 2 ft, to make vertical wall sections. But
the effectiveness of this will depend on the overhead treatment
of the stage. A curtain set usually includes borders, and these
reduce vertical height. I hate borders of this sort. I prefer to
have all the backstage area of the theatre painted black,
including the ceiling and any overhead grid work. If backstage working lights are shone only where required, provided
the stage is lit with spotlights and not floods or battens, borders
are not necessary. For many years the old Questors Theatre
has been exemplary from this point of view, and I do not know
why so many backstage walls are painted a clinical white—
which is just about the worst colour for them. In the theatre
we have to deal with, the backstage area is a heterogeneous

mess. This means we can paint bits of the back wall without upsetting anyone. But it also means that borders must be used. It is a good idea to keep people's eyes away from the ceiling. So that the author's requirements cannot be precisely carried out. In fact the best way of getting the sense of a yawning crack may be to paint the back wall white rather than black, after all!

I am not quite sure how to treat the third play. The two boxes are quite straightforward, though they are supposed to contain some substantial paraphernalia including an umbrella and a coke brazier. It may be necessary to bring these props on from offstage, though an umbrella could be coped with easily enough if the box were a chest about 18 in. × 18 in. and about 3 ft 3 in. long. A man's umbrella is usually just over three feet long. A folding umbrella could be used, but this would spoil the prosaic quality required when the umbrella is produced. The brazier may be more difficult. There is a very small brazier used by riveters, though it is clearly not what the author had in mind. These are matters for the producer to sort out, and he can deal with them according to his wishes. It is the progress of the scene that is our main concern. The house is not in a good condition to start with—"You've got some nasty cracks in your plaster," says the workman. And when the house is finished, it is finished in the emptiest sense of the word. Every time I read this bit of the play, I am filled with a huge, awful sense of emptiness. Perhaps this is a clue. I don't want to put on stage the doorways suggested by the author. The two boxes and the actors are enough. Anything important about the house is fully conveyed in the dialogue and the sound effects. If the producer agrees, I suggest that we provide the two boxes only, leaving an entrance at either side of the stage through the curtains. Lighting will play a very important part. The actors must be very brightly lit at the beginning. There are effects suggested by the author for the birthday sequence—but we shall probably isolate the characters in a single spotlight apiece without using colour—and towards the end of the play, a dim and shadowy light is required.

For the last play all that is required, in our surround of black curtains, is a suggestion of fallen blocks and masonry. Some small rostrum blocks from stock, painted broken grey, will

serve. We must compose with them an arrangement that
enables the two characters to sit in isolation, or close together.
The emphasis must be central, and different heights will help
to get a haphazard effect. It might be helpful to take a six-foot
flat put it on its side, and sketch a ruined vista using black and
grey paint. But the locale is brilliantly indicated in the
dialogue—

GIRL: Is this Hyde Park Corner?
PHYTHICK: Piccadilly Circus.
GIRL: It's changed.

This understatement would be spoiled by too much attention
to painting a background.

There are no particular difficulties in construction or
painting. The setting plan must be carefully prepared, and the
curtains examined. It is important to see that the tracks are
secure and well lubricated. I like curtains to be suspended so
that they just touch the floor. If they have been running too
fully on the floor the bottom chain may wear through the
material and this must be attended to. If they have been kept
clear of the floor they will probably gather unwanted movement
and may reveal the feet of actors and staff backstage. Where a
curtain surround is used as a negative background, as in this
production, it is important to be able to keep the curtains open
so that they provide easy entrances and exits. There is nothing
more annoying to an audience than an actor brushing aside the
curtains for his exit. Our imaginations can stand so much, but
probably not flagrant opposition from a contrary reality;
worse still, of course, if actors cannot find the hidden gap and
have to fight their way on or off through a jungle of drapery.
This is an effect that may have its place in another sort of
production!

The second production of *The Lunatic View* is to be done by a
small professional company, which has a theatre in the round.
In fact this play was first performed in the theatre in the round
set up by my company at 41 Fitzroy Square in London. There
is no theatre in the round, properly built as such, in England.
And the difficulties of staging at Fitzroy Square were considerable. There was virtually no backstage space for storing props
or scenery, and very little accommodation for actors. However,
the lighting could be set with relative ease and the hall provided

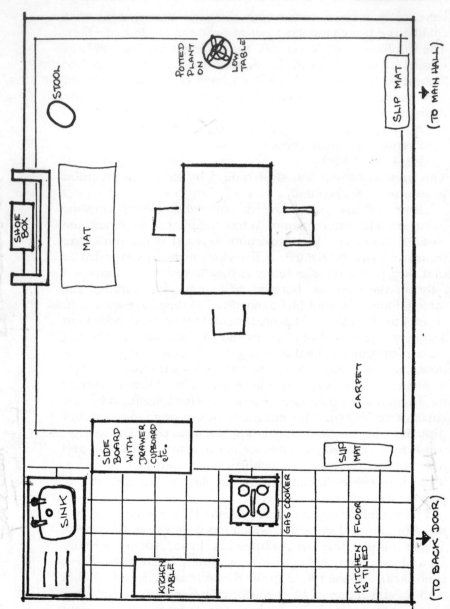

FIG. 43. Ground-plan for *The Birthday Party* by Harold Pinter, who Produced his own Play for the Studio, The 1928 Company, Twi 1pme, N. the Round

an acting area of 18 ft × 24 ft, with three access points at
floor-level. The building, designed for the Y.M.C.A. as the
Indian student's hostel, and the hall, called after Mahatma
Gandhi, have an attractive appearance. But it was never
intended that plays should be staged there, though there is a
tiny platform stage, far too small for staging plays, but quite
suitable as a lecture or recital platform. The hall can be used
as a theatre in the round provided the company brings in
rostrum units to raise the rows of seats.

In these circumstances it is easy to see how quickly the
designer can prepare for this play. The play does not require
much scenery and the hall cannot cope with it. This is a nice
concatenation of clues. The key to design lies in the setting for
"Memento Mori," which demanded the most elaborate treatment in the production already discussed. When you think
about it, you suddenly realize that once the convention of no
scenery is established, the performance of "Memento Mori" is
going to be glorious. The action takes place in an empty room.
The fireplace and the sliding doors on the cupboards can all be
imaginary. This will give the actors scope for skilful mime.
The audience will actually see the old man struggling inside
the cupboard while the young man searches for the secret
button, and so on. Each of the other plays can be set with the
furniture or blocks already envisaged, but no other scenery is
required. And, of course, the false proscenium will be of no
use. Strangely enough, though, the idea of doing the play in
black and white lingers on. It still helps give a unifying style
to the play. However, the occasional dash of colour may be
helpful, particularly in such details as the flower and the
knitting in "Getting and Spending." It is important to work
out a careful series of ground plans, and it becomes apparent
that the boxes used as *his* and *hers* can be used again as masonry
in the final play, "Then." These matters increasingly trespass
on the producer's territory.

"The Birthday Party" Designed for Theatre in the Round

I have found it best for the producer to design his own setting
when working in theatre in the round. I have seldom designed
a setting for another producer, except when he has had little
experience outside the enclosed stage. This was the case when

Harold Pinter produced his own play *The Birthday Party*, for which I drew a ground-plan, leaving details to him. There is a danger that people will think that a theatre-in-the-round production, since it cannot involve conventional quantities of scenery, needs no designing whatever. Certainly a scenic designer may feel that this form of theatre makes him redundant. To some extent this is true. As I have already said, it is preferable for the producer and designer to be the same person. But the design still needs careful attention. Let me briefly describe two further productions of plays in a theatre in the round, from the designer's standpoint.

A Play in a Single Room—"In Camera"

In Camera, translated from *Huis Clos* by Sartre, is a particularly fascinating play. The action takes place in a single room, without windows. The door opens to let people in, but when they want to get out it is locked fast and when they don't want to get out it is easily opened. Into this room come three people and here they will serve their time, forever, in hell, a hell of their own creating. For each turns to one other for help, and is rejected, while despising—hating rather—the third person. This is the vicious circle. They are each other's torturers. There can surely be no better way to stage this play than in a theatre in the round. During the action of the play, each of the characters is given moments of vision when what is happening to earthly companions can be seen. In the film, made from the play, these visions were translated into actuality by making use of a screen (with an invisible projector). But in the play they depend on verbal description. In the production that I prepared in Scarborough in 1960, three chairs were set round a circle of white. The rest of the floor was black. The circle was slightly off-centre, to allow for a table on which the bronze atrocity was set, and this table itself was slightly off the centre line to leave a balancing space for the entry. The white circle was treated as a sort of forbidden ground, and the actors moved round it except for their moments of vision; then they stood centrally on the white area which was strongly illuminated from profile spots. The lighting gave an eerie appearance to the actor, who seemed almost to be floating in limbo for a moment. Then back to the circle of attraction and rejection as the characters moved from chair to chair in desperation and loathing.

"Rashomon"—A Different Approach to Design

A completely different approach to setting a play for theatre in the round is exemplified in a production of *Rashomon* that I saw at the Alley Theatre in Houston, Texas. Although the building was originally intended for other purposes, it has been carefully and thoroughly adapted as a theatre in the round, dealing sensibly with whatever snags were offered by the structure. For *Rashomon* the whole auditorium was festooned with liana and hanging branches. These were mostly just above head level so that the audience was not impeded in finding seats, nor in seeing the actors. But the actors were seen through a framework of green leaves, giving the impression of a forest. Spotlights sent beams through the leaves to give a wonderfully broken texture of illumination on the actors. There has to be a fairly large and clear acting area for the vigorous action of the play and I can think of no better way of setting it. For this production, use was made of a small side stage which housed the characters beneath the gate I suppose it need hardly be mentioned that the whole of the auditorium had to be painted (I suspect it was black but I can't remember) to allow the wholesale illusion to have its impact. Unfortunately this scenic treatment is not available to a company like my own which makes use of other people's halls for short periods at a time on condition that we do not spoil the existing décor! Further, the Fire Officer may raise difficulties. And though I welcome simplicity of staging this does not mean that everything should be dull, and the sort of treatment given to *Rashomon* was glorious and, I think, fundamentally simple for all that.

A Familiar Play—"An Inspector Calls"

For my next example, let me take a more familiar play. The acting edition of *An Inspector Calls*, by J. B. Priestley, gives the following information—

> The three acts, which are continuous, take place in the dining-room of the Birling's house in Brumley, an industrial city of the North Midlands. An evening in spring, 1912.

Note. This acting edition follows the original script of the play, in which one set was used throughout. In the New Theatre production different aspects of the room were shown in each of the three acts. For the benefit of those companies whose scenic facilities will permit, Ground Plans and a Furniture Plot prepared in accordance with this scheme are given at the end of the book.

I find this very interesting. The play is a straightforward story, with slight mystical overtones, showing how the apparently respectable and ordinary members of a good middle-class family are all involved, more or less culpably, in the

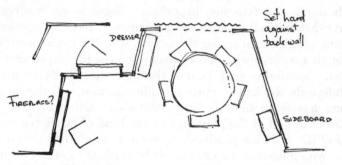

Fig. 44. Sketch Ground-plan for *An Inspector Calls* by J. B. Priestley at the Frinton Summer Theatre

unpleasant suicide of a young woman. Each member of the family is exposed in turn as a sham. The play is carefully set in a period when the unsinkable *Titanic* was about to be launched and when the Great War was shortly to come and destroy almost everything of value in a society that felt secure. The irony is nice. As in any good play, it is the characters that count for most. Acting is the essence of drama. Plot and ethics are less important, and the background is of subsidiary importance. From the scenic designer's point of view this may sound as though I am suggesting that any old décor will do. This is not so. But the décor must be subsidiary, and it must be right. I imagine this play has been produced in thousands of different theatres and on open stages as well as enclosed stages, and I dare say there are thousands of different ways of doing the setting right. But I read into the note quoted above the implication that it is an advantage to have scenic facilities that will permit the setting to be moved around. And for the life of me I don't see why. The play is set in the dining-room of the Birlings' house, a fairly large suburban house that is conventional and well built. The play begins with the family round the dining table, having just finished a good dinner, and as the action progresses the family move away from the table. Moving the set may help to emphasize this change of locale, but, I suspect, it may equally draw attention to the inherent unlikelihood of the action being confined to the dining-room anyhow. The author suggests that the action is continuous and I think the play should be acted straight through without an interval. But for various reasons that have little to do with theatre, intervals are usually inflicted on any play of more than an hour's duration, and if, as is likely, intervals are observed in *An Inspector Calls*, there is surely no excuse for not shifting the scene into the drawing-room or the study if scenery is to be shifted at all. It seems to me that the note really means something like this—

If you don't understand this play and expect to communicate your boredom to the audience, a large stage might be helpful as you can then have fun with the scenery (in spite of the author's intentions) and you need have no talent for design as long as you can keep things on the move, and occupy a lot of space.

Limitations of Space

My reaction may be grossly unfair, but I do think that it is all too common for people to suppose that a small stage is a bad thing, whereas in fact a small stage is more often than not a good thing (taking large and small within reasonable limits either way) and gives tremendous scope for good design. The great danger of starting off with a big stage is that you feel an urge to fill it. The result may be a bit absurd, as for instance when *Sailor Beware* was staged in London and the parlour of a working-class terrace house appeared on the stage with walls as high as a mansion and enough furniture to fill a small house. But this absurdity can be forgiven—and we are so used to it in big theatres that it almost passes unobserved—though it is more difficult to forgive the company that presents this play

Fig. 45. Rough Sketch for *An Inspector Calls*, at the Frinton Summer Theatre, Designed and Produced by Stephen Joseph

on a small stage and attempts to copy the London setting. This
is absurdity squared and beyond lunacy! So with *An Inspector
Calls* rejoice if you have a small stage. The important items of
setting are the door, the table carrying the remains of a good
meal, chairs and a telephone. These items should be combined
in an atmosphere of security, prosperity and sobriety belonging
to the period. Ingenuity may devise ways of using the set
ironically and I have heard of a production where the walls
become increasingly transparent as the rottenness of the characters was revealed until walls and people were naked to their
rotten cores. This sounds promising. But the play does not
progress quite so simply. For a moment, towards the end of
the play, an attempt is made to laugh the whole revelation off.
Material reality asserts itself, and the final twist is sudden,
subtle and, I suspect, not entirely convincing. So there is a risk
here that a scenic device will expose a weakness in the play even
though it seems a remarkably appropriate device. In a small
theatre the set can be better treated with simplicity.

It is worth, perhaps, going to an absolute extreme to show
how *An Inspector Calls* can be set on a tiny stage—a stage too
small for comfort as far as a play is concerned. The theatre is a
Women's Institute hall. It is long and narrow. A platform
has been erected at one end of the hall, thus losing height, and,
as there is a simple gable roof, any flying is out of the question.
There is virtually no wing space, no backstage space of any
sort, and no clever idea to give any sort of reprieve. The theatre
has a stock of flats, eight feet tall, but most of them are plain
flats, and, since we are working for a small professional repertory
company, all the flats are in use either for this week's play or
next week's. It is important to give as large an acting area as
possible, to suggest that the room, although primarily a dining-
room, can be used for general purposes, and that it is simple and
solid. It is probably wise to set the door with adjacent flats at a
good angle so as to get maximum solidity and strength, and, at
the same time, leave room offstage for actors to prepare for
their entrances. The ground-plan (*see* page 108) is simple
enough but clearly shows the limitations of space. A rough
perspective sketch goes further and reveals its inadequacies
immediately. It really is out of proportion—the furniture looks
much too big—quite apart from any weaknesses in the design

itself. But there it is, and it was the best I could do at the time
—and in the time, limited since I was producing the play
myself.

I think the idea for the setting is sensible enough, but I
would have liked a slightly bigger stage after all. Few companies will have to work in a space as small as this.

Limitations of Expense

Sometimes, of course, the main limitation is not space but
money. I once did a production for Jack Rodney's London
Theatre Group on the fringe of the Edinburgh Festival. The
play was C. E. Webber's *The Mortal Bard*. It is a delightful
play, and the action moves fluidly from one scene to another.
The playwright had already written other plays which clearly
demanded the use of a large revolving stage. But St. Mary's
Hall, where the play was to be presented, did not have a
revolving stage and we could certainly not afford to install one.
In fact the production budget was £5. We possessed no scenery
whatever. However, we borrowed a few rostrums, 3 ft × 6 ft
× 1 ft and a large number of baby spots; we hired some curtains (our rashest expenditure), and the stage manager helped
me build the set of 2-in. × 1-in. batten and string. The areas
representing different scenes were marked by the use of
different levels and by string walls. The string formed an
almost opaque background when the lights were on the downstage side of it, but, when the actors were lit from upstage, the
string disappeared. This is an effect familiar from using gauzes.
The hired curtains were used as traverse curtains, immediately
upstage of the main curtains, and they were chosen so that
shadows could be projected on them from upstage in a scene
taking place at a dance. The play was witty and ingenuous,
the acting was full of fun and vigour, and I believe that the
string caught the spirit of the production very well. It is worth
emphasizing that the set would simply not have worked without
a precise and careful use of spotlights.

So much for my own work. It will be refreshing now to take
a look at the work of other designers who have dealt with small
theatres.

IX

STAGE SETTINGS

DESIGNERS are usually very busy people and few of them find time to write about their work. And the theatre is an ephemeral business. Not many people are interested in yesterday's plays and settings (though historical research gives respectability to productions of many years ago). In most theatres no photographic records are kept of settings, and sketches and plans are soon destroyed. However, I have made a collection of photographs that show settings in small theatres; most of them are of recent date and all of them are from theatres in England. Some very good settings photograph badly, and making a selection has not been easy.

Plate V

(*Upper*) Plates V–VIII show settings for very small stages. The Barn Theatre, at Dartington Hall, has a narrow span, about 23 ft 6 in., and virtually no wing space. However, the stage is 42 ft deep and, in the setting for *Moon in the Yellow River*, Reece Pemberton has used the depth to make an interesting setting. Steps and raised levels at the back help to avoid masking. Producer, Miriam Adams.

(*Lower*) The amateur Village Players at Great Hucklow have, under the direction of L. du Garde Peach, earned a reputation throughout Derbyshire and neighbouring counties for their dialect comedies and for the excellence of costumes and settings in these and all their productions. Although the stage is only 20 ft across, it has a depth of 30 ft—a feature well used here. The simplicity of this setting for Shaw's *Captain Brassbound's Conversion* gives a feeling of spaciousness. The columns are three-dimensional and the backcloth is well enough lit to give a good sense of distance.

Plate VI

(*Upper*)   This shows a setting at the Frinton Summer Theatre.
The proscenium opening is 17 ft 6 in., the stage depth
14 ft, and there are stairs and other hazards backstage.
The theatre is in an ordinary Women's Institute Hall.
The erection of the stage was an afterthought and
there is no extra head-room. The setting is for a
farce by Roy Russel called *Return to Bedlam*. A staircase is very important. Here, the turning toward the
audience is merely painted—and the flats screwed to
the roof. The borders are untidy, and there is too
much furniture, but the setting reveals some ingenuity
(my own) if not much else.

(*Lower*)   The box set can be twisted to give a view into the
corner of a room, as here designed by Disley Jones
for Act I in Walter Hudd's production of *Penelope*
by Maugham at the Arts Theatre, London. The
designer has obviously taken great care—and had
some fun—in selecting dressing such as the standard
lamp and shade, the bric-à-brac on the mantelpiece,
and the pictures on the wall; the window is splendid!

Plate VII

(*Upper*)   There are several ways of coping in a small theatre
with plays that demand several changes of setting.
At the Arts Theatre in London, Disley Jones made
use of a semi-permanent set for Peter Hall's production of *The Impresario from Smyrna* by Goldoni. It is
stylishly painted—including the floor—and use is
made of a cyclorama, with a groundrow to give
distance.

(*Lower*)   Furniture and two flown units quickly give a character to one of several scenes from *The Impresario
from Smyrna* each of which makes use of the permanent
setting.

Plate VIII

(*Upper*)   Where there is very little overhead space, as at the
Library Theatre in Manchester, good use can be
made of skeleton sets. For David Scase's production

of *Mandragola* by Machiavelli, Daphne Hart has designed a formal setting, with clean, simple lines and forced perspectives that suggest the street scenes of Serlio and the early Italian theatre.

(*Middle*) For *An Inspector Calls* by Priestley at the Library Theatre, Jennifer Wyatt's skeleton set reveals in silhouette the crowded industrial background, contrasting with the wealthy interior—a good statement of one of the play's intentions.

(*Lower*) An interesting setting for Lorca's *Blood Wedding*, making use of simple shapes in different planes, and depending on a good cyclorama. Another example of Daphne Hart's original approach to the problems and opportunities of the Library Theatre, Manchester.

Plate IX

(*Upper*) Many amateur companies work with curtain settings, against which scenic units can be placed. An ingenious example at the Little Theatre in Lewes shows a large arch used as a semi-permanent setting for Masefield's *The Witch*.

(*Lower*) Another scene from *The Witch*. The furniture has been changed, and the cloth behind the arch which remains with the curtains throughout the play. Note that a candelabra has been flown in for this scene. The floor has been effectively tiled.

Plate X

(*Upper*) The Moot House Players in Harlow do not have their own theatre. Many of their productions are done on an open stage—or a three-sided arena—as here. The setting for *The Cherry Orchard* is extremely simple and evocative; designed by Gordon and Bettina Hewlett, it explores the three-dimensional acting space sensitively and with economy.

(*Lower*) Theatre in the round depends almost entirely on furniture for its scenic effect. Here, for Shaw's *The Man of Destiny*, the furniture is simple, country stuff, and even the floor is negatively untidy—but it sets

off the costumed actors very well. The production,
by Peter Cheeseman, is from the Library Theatre,
Scarborough.

Plate XI

(*Upper*) The box set is still the commonest demand made on
the designer. The amateur Tavistock Repertory
Company at the Tower Theatre in London staged a
notable production of Harold Pinter's *The Birthday
Party*. The set by John Crisp is helped considerably
by a basically simple and realistic approach with
atmospheric lighting. Note the effective brick wall
backing outside the window.

(*Lower*) The repertory company at the Ipswich Theatre
staged *The Gazebo*, by Alec Coppel, with this delightful set, which is rich in good detail, down to the
floor. Produced by Robert Chetwyn and designed
by Juanita Waterson, this is a good example of a
straightforward box set done with freshness and
enjoyment.

Plate XII

(*Upper*) *A Man for all Seasons*, by Robert Bolt, demands something unusual as setting. For the production by
David Phethean at the Queen's Theatre, Hornchurch,
the designer, Pelo Cumpston, has built an intriguing
set using chicken-wire and tubular scaffold and a
raked timber floor. The formal shapes and symbols
are nicely evocative, and the different levels, simply
achieved, are very useful. In this photograph the
crown has been spotlit, and lighting will play a large
part in focusing attention on this "busy" set.

(*Lower*) *Oh Brother!* by Glyn Jones, produced by Robert
Chetwyn at the Arts Theatre, Ipswich, and designed
by Juanita Waterson. Use is made of a number of
different materials—from wire fencing to conventional flats—and the fully three-dimensional effect
depends for its success on such details as the round
window (carefully lit), and a well lit sky-cloth. The

SET FOR *Moon in the Yellow River*, THE BARN THEATRE, DARTINGTON HALL

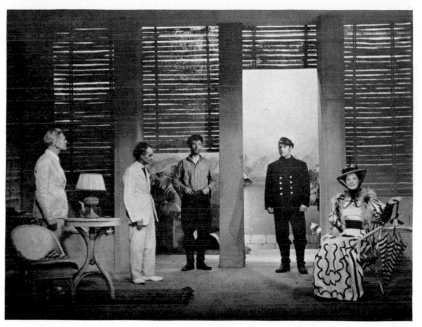

SETTING FOR SHAW'S *Captain Brassbound's Conversion*

PLATE V

Return to Bedlam AT THE FRINTON SUMMER THEATRE

SETTING BY DISLEY JONES FOR MAUGHAM'S *Penelope* AT
THE ARTS THEATRE, LONDON

PLATE VI

The Impresario from Smyrna—Permanent Setting, The Arts Theatre, London

The Impresario from Smyrna—as Above with the Addition of some Furniture
and Flown Units

PLATE VII

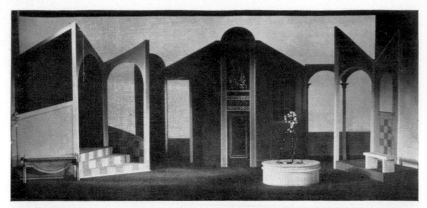

(*Upper*) SKELETON SETTING FOR *Mandragola* AT THE LIBRARY THEATRE, MANCHESTER
(*Middle*) SET FOR *An Inspector Calls* AT THE LIBRARY THEATRE, MANCHESTER
(*Lower*) SETTING FOR LORCA'S *Blood Wedding* AT THE LIBRARY THEATRE, MANCHESTER

PLATE VIII

SETTING FOR MASEFIELD'S *The Witch* AT THE LITTLE THEATRE, LEWES

ANOTHER SCENE FOR *The Witch*

PLATE IX

ARENA SETTING FOR *The Cherry Orchard* PRESENTED BY THE MOOT HOUSE
PLAYERS, HARLOW

PRODUCTION IN THE ROUND OF *The Man of Destiny*, THE LIBRARY THEATRE,
SCARBOROUGH

PLATE X

The Birthday Party STAGED BY THE AMATEUR TAVISTOCK REPERTORY COMPANY AT THE TOWER THEATRE, LONDON

The Gazebo, SETTING AT THE ARTS THEATRE, IPSWICH

PLATE XI

A Man for all Seasons AT THE QUEEN'S THEATRE, HORNCHURCH

Oh Brother! PRODUCTION AT THE ARTS THEATRE, IPSWICH

PLATE XII

(*Upper*) SETTING FOR *Separate Rooms* AT THE OLDHAM THEATRE CLUB
(*Middle*) BRENDAN BEHAN'S *Hostage* AT THE OLDHAM THEATRE CLUB
(*Lower*) SPLIT SETTING FOR *The Hamlet of Stepney Green* AT THE OLDHAM
THEATRE CLUB

PLATE XIII

Arsenic and Old Lace, The Guildford Repertory Theatre

The Imaginary Invalid at the Playhouse, Sheffield

PLATE XIV

Kill Two Birds, Setting at the Leatherhead Repertory
Theatre Club

Sparrers Can't Sing at the Royal Theatre, Lincoln

PLATE XV

True Love or the Bloomer AT THE PLAYHOUSE, SHEFFIELD

THE PLAYHOUSE, SHEFFIELD, PRODUCTION OF *The Iron Harp*

PLATE XVI

stage at the Ipswich Theatre is only 20 ft × 16 ft, and lack of height means resorting to borders (here a bit unsatisfactory).

Plate XIII

(*Upper*) On a bigger stage, Carl Paulson, director of productions at the Oldham Theatre Club, has produced *Separate Rooms* by Alan Dinehart; designer, Trevor Trueman. The clean, square, formal lines of the set catch characteristics of modern interior decoration, and the skyscraper sky line is very effective.

(*Middle*) A nice feeling of chaos is conveyed by the angled lines of Trevor Trueman's setting for Brendan Behan's *The Hostage* at the same theatre. Rough surface textures and ill-assorted furniture echo the disorganized patches of light.

(*Lower*) The split setting for *Hamlet of Stepney Green* by Bernard Kops at the Oldham Theatre Club depends a good deal on the right choice of furniture, and is here helped by carpet and painted floorcloth. Tops of the flats have been shaded to help focus down on the actors and to break the height of the wall frieze.

Plate XIV

(*Upper*) *Arsenic and Old Lace* by Kesselring at the Guildford Repertory Theatre, produced by Harry Lomax, designer Ian Knight. There is a good clutter here, and some excellent props and furniture have been collected, notably the pictures, chairs, table cloths, staircarpet and the all-important chest. The staircase is ambitious and effective.

(*Lower*) Where a black curtain surround is available, stylized profiles can be used to catch a period flavour. Geoffrey Ost, director of productions at the Playhouse, Sheffield, has set *The Imaginary Invalid* by Molière in a highly artificial enclosure of cut down flats; the books and props and even the centre chandelier are painted flat. The downstage doors are solid, with solid mouldings, to try and recapture the value of eighteenth-century proscenium doors.

Plate XV

(*Upper*) Leatherhead Repertory Theatre Club presented *Kill Two Birds* by Philip Levene, designed by Sidney Lewis, with a nicely cluttered set where props and furniture give the locale. The box is broken by dividing the acting area into two spaces.

(*Lower*) The Royal Theatre at Lincoln does not have a big stage; but the space has been well used in Suzanne Billing's design for *Sparrers Can't Sing* by Stephen Lewis. The play was first presented by Theatre Workshop at the Theatre Royal, Stratford, with setting by John Bury whose influence can be clearly seen—certainly the angle of the set is much the same. But the detail and texture are original and excellent. The setting is greatly helped by good lighting which keeps attention in the centre of the space and leaves out of our notice what happens beyond the boundaries of the proscenium frame.

Plate XVI

(*Upper*) Geoffrey Ost's setting for *True Love, or the Bloomer*, by C. Neilson Gatty and Z. Bramley Moore, at the Playhouse, Sheffield, is not only interestingly shaped, but has some most effective painting. Wallpaper, frieze and dado, each calling for a different sort of brushwork, are excellent, and the marble pillars, solid and shiny, are superb. Note the carefully chosen furniture, curtains, pictures and mirror. The steps to the doorway on stage right enable the designer to effect a sleight of hand and, by using a balcony rail and well-designed backing, place the room convincingly upstairs.

(*Lower*) *The Iron Harp*, by Joseph O'Connor, another example of Geoffrey Ost's fine craftsmanship at The Playhouse, Sheffield. Floor and walls for a convincing room. The lighting is carefully used to keep attention

on the actors and the top of walls fades into darkness.
Furniture and properties are well chosen and the
total effect is highly satisfying.

When you have looked at these pictures, I hope you will
want to see more books on scenic design; and there are many
of them by better qualified persons than myself—people with
more experience, more talent and, indeed, better writers.
After this chapter I have put a list of books that I am particularly fond of. But more important, I hope that reading this
book has stimulated you to action, as a designer, as a theatre-
goer and as an eager spectator to the background of life. In
this book I may have let too much of "the background of life"
into the business of scenery; you will certainly have noticed
some highly personal statements. You may accept or reject
my prejudices, but I hope you will share my love of the theatre.
You may have noted my preoccupation with the open stage,
and particularly with theatre in the round. Is it fair to offer
the excuse that I have dragged it in if only to help redress the
balance which weighs so heavily at present in favour of the
enclosed stage? The theatre should be not one thing, but many
things. There is no one right form of theatre. There is no
straightforward evolution of theatrical form. Many forms of
theatre are valid, and we should have and enjoy many forms.
A man with a limited taste may be no more than a limited man.
I cannot accept the weakness implied by such limitation. Then
again, simplicity appeals to me because it can carry so much
strength. I like technical efficiency, and deplore the lack of it
in our theatre—particularly as far as actual buildings are
concerned. A theatre of no matter what form should be a
place where the audience can see and hear actors acting. The
argument between the advocates of different theatre forms has
often become confused with the argument over efficiency, and
too many theatres are built where the audience cannot see or
hear properly, but apparently no one cares much about this
as long as there is (or is not!) a proscenium arch. . . . The
scene designer inevitably gets involved in the quarrel, because
an ill-equipped theatre usually makes his work more difficult
than it should be. But the designer and all other technicians
must do their best. We are there to help the actors. The

drama is a passionate affair between actors and audiences. It is a glorious affair, revealing the deepest mysteries of human behaviour, and satisfying the deepest hungers of the human spirit—universal mysteries and universal hungers. I sometimes think that laughter and applause in a theatre are the most jubilant sounds in the universe, staking mankind's claim to continued existence. And, at least, I am glad to be a worker, in no matter how small a way, in such a business.

BIBLIOGRAPHY

HERE is a highly selective list of books. It is limited by the fact that I have recommended only those books that I have read again and again either with real pleasure or for the information they contain. Obviously there are many books that have never come to my attention and the list reflects the limitations of my own reading. I have sometimes chosen one out of several books dealing with the same subject (particularly the history of the theatre in general) even when they are all enjoyable. There are also many books that I simply don't like enough to recommend them. I have divided the list into different categories, hoping that this will serve as a guide, and have made comments that may help in selection. Such a personal approach to a bibliography is necessarily open to criticism, but I am not attempting to indicate the sources of my own ideas (though each of these books has taught me something more or less) so much as trying to egg the reader on to further reading.

I have mentioned more books by Richard Southern than any other single author. There is no need to apologize for this. He is probably the greatest theatre scholar living in this country at the present time, and his books are always richly rewarding. Sometimes he verges towards the academic, and sometimes he tends to a journalistic style, but he has the theatre first and foremost in his mind—indeed, he writes and works and seems to live theatre! In a country where there is almost no tradition of scholarship in the theatre (apart from the study of playwrights and plays as literary phenomena) his must have been a lonely path, and as a pioneer he has had to face extraordinary problems. This accounts for the varying treatment he has given the different topics in his many books (some of which are outside the scope of our subject and are therefore not mentioned here). But I have enjoyed them all (even when they have made me angry —very enjoyable at such times), and the recurrence of his name in the list below is some sort of salute to his importance.

You may also notice that there are a number of books by American writers. This follows from the fact that so many people in America are interested in the study of theatre, thanks, largely, to their numerous drama departments in universities. But the American theatre itself is young and still very dependent on European traditions. So most of these American books deal considerably with European drama, and can be safely recommended to any reader.

Theatre History

Each of the following three books deals with the whole history of the theatre, and each has some emphasis on the practical business of staging plays and avoids over emphasis on the more common material of dramatic literature.

LAVER, JAMES, *Drama: its Costume and Décor* (Studio).
Laver is an expert on costume and a keen historian of the theatre.
The book tells the story of the scenic theatre in a delightfully argu-
mentative way; it is easy to follow, and very well illustrated.
MACGOWAN, KENNETH and MELNITZ, WILLIAM, *The Living Stage* (Prentice-
Hall).
The book surveys the history of theatre all over the world. It is a good
introduction, and puts forward accepted ideas rather than novel
points of view. Its wide scope is its main recommendation. Illustrations originate from equally wide sources, and there are useful little
tables of dates. It is, of course, an American book, and the final
chapters have an American bias.
SOUTHERN, RICHARD, *The Seven Ages of Theatre* (Faber & Faber).
The author chooses certain periods and certain places (widely distributed over the world) to show different aspects of staging and
scenic presentation. He gives particular attention to the interlude of
Tudor times, and, finally, he is clearly enamoured of the open stage.
But the book remains a great plea for all sorts of theatre, using all sorts
of conventions.

The Scenic Theatre

These three books deal with the development of the scenic theatre, or
the proscenium theatre, that is still our main concern today.
LAWRENSON, T. E., *The French Stage in the Seventeenth Century* (Manchester
University Press).
This is a scholarly book, dealing with the impact of Renaissance concepts of theatre and scenic presentation, as developed in Italy, on
French theatre. In France ballet was the court entertainment at this
time, and the great playwrights Molière, Corneille and Racine, faced
a theatre that was derived from Greek via misunderstandings of Italian
scholars who were more concerned with moving pictures and opera
than with plays! It is a key dilemma, anticipating the present-day
dissatisfaction with the picture-frame stage. There are interesting
reproductions of scenic designs and theatre plans.
SOUTHERN, RICHARD, *Changeable Scenery* (Faber & Faber).
This is a book for the scholar and the connoisseur. It traces the start
of the scenic theatre in England with Inigo Jones, and follows its
development to the period in the middle of the nineteenth century when
techniques of presentation became more or less crystallized into the
form familiar at the present time. The book is nicely illustrated, and
absolutely thorough in its research.
WORSTHORNE, S. T., *Venetian Opera in the Seventeenth Century* (Oxford).
Although this is a scholarly book, I think it can be read with delight
by anyone interested in the origins of our own theatre. It deals only
with the theatres of Venice and much of the book is concerned with the
musical score and musical conventions of opera, but there are many
delightful quotations from eye-witness accounts of scenery at work in

the theatre. There are also excellent reproductions of designs, including pairs showing designs of scenery and the machinery required to work it. The book is beautifully printed and presented.

Scenery

Here are half a dozen books dealing with scenic design during the early part of this century. Each of these books is full of illustrations that have an immediate relationship with our own theatre.

FUERST and HUME, *Twentieth-century Stage Decoration* (two volumes) (Knopf). The first volume of text serves to date the book (1928) but the second volume consists of half-tone illustrations of stage settings from Europe and America, forming an invaluable record of a vigorous period in scene design. If you want to know what the designers of the last generation or so were doing, you will find examples of nearly all the great artists, as well as many others, reproduced here.

GORELIK, MORDECAI, *New Theatres for Old* (Dennis Dobson Ltd.). As long as you are not put off by the capsule headings (in the style of an American news magazine), this book is full of good argument. It is not exactly a history, but it deals with all sorts of historical techniques of presentation as well as the theatre of modern times. It is a good expression of the unease which designers feel when faced with the conflicting demands of realism and illusion—of truth and convention. There are excellent illustrations showing some very exciting stage settings, as well as portraits of producers and theorists of the drama. The book ends on a note of excitement and looking forward—it was first published in 1940—and is refreshingly uncomplacent.

HOLME, GEOFFREY, *Design in the Theatre* (Studio). Most of the introductory material is complacent or pompous, but there are plenty of illustrations of costume and scene designs. Among the illustrations are some brilliant ones, but many of the designs give the impression that the British Theatre of the twenties and thirties must have confined its scenic artists in a rarified and arty atmosphere. It is worth being aware of this!

LAMBOURNE, NORAH, *Staging the Play* (Studio). This is a modest and very practical book. Its scope is limited, but it goes into detail, so that it is an excellent book for the beginner. There are good illustrations and drawings.

MOUSSINAC, LEON, *The New Movement in the Theatre* (Batsford). Published in 1931, this magnificent book deals with the European theatre of the previous ten years. The bulk of the volume consists of coloured illustrations of sets and costumes, designs and photographs of actual settings. The so-called "new movement" did not have much effect in this country until it had passed through the eager hands of American artists. The book takes us back to roots and is a valid source of inspiration even today.

SIMONSON, LEE, *The Stage is Set* (Dover Publications). First published in 1932, this book by one of America's most interesting scenic artists is full of turbulent thought about the development of the scenic theatre. He is concerned in tracing the elements that have made the modern scenic artist what he is today, and the book really warms up in dealing with Saxe-Meiningen, Appia and Craig. There are many good illustrations, including some of the author's own excellent designs.

Practical Books

Here are books that tell you how to do it—or, at least, how it is done—ranging from drawing to lighting, and from making to painting scenery.

BENTHAM, FREDERICK, *Stage Lighting* (Pitman).
Here is an absolutely thorough and practical book about stage lighting. It goes into technical details, and also deals wisely with general problems of lighting as they face the producer in different theatres. The book is well illustrated with drawings, diagrams and reproductions of stage sets showing lighting effects.

FORMAN, ROBERT, *Over the Drawing Board* (Cleaver-Hume Press).
Primarily intended for the draughtsman, this is a guide to using the drawing board, techniques of layout and perspective, and certain details of architectural planning. Although not aimed at the scene designer, I think this is an ideal companion for anyone who enjoys using drawing instruments.

GILLETTE, A. S., *Stage Scenery* (Harper).
An American book which sets out to deal with the scenic demands of a typical university theatre. (Yes, there are over a hundred universities in the U.S.A. with drama departments!) But there is a vast amount of material that will interest any scenic artist. There are details of scenic construction from the simplest of flats to the most complicated three-dimensional pieces. It is a book for the careful and thorough worker.

MELVILL, HARALD, *Designing and Painting Scenery* (Art Trade Press).
This is the best book I know on the actual business of scene-painting. It goes into more detail than I do in the present volume, and it is illustrated with many examples of straightforward sets that have been used in repertory and touring theatres. The author is not concerned with historical background, nor with any theatre other than the conventional picture-frame stage. He concentrates on the practical processes of getting sets painted. My own copy is splashed with scene-paint; there can be no greater compliment!

McCANDLESS, STANLEY, *A Method of Lighting the Stage* (Theatre Art Books).
This is a very useful book. It outlines a simple system for using spot-lights so that the stage can be well lit for any play. Over this basic lighting alterations can be made to suit the particular play and production. The system can grow into a complex scheme for lighting an elaborate production; but this shows the strength of the system—which, at its simplest, can be understood by anyone. It is an American book, and the instruments described (and the terminology used) are American. It is not difficult, however, to find the equivalent English apparatus.

SOUTHERN, RICHARD, *Proscenium and Sight-lines* (Faber & Faber).
In a very thorough and painstaking manner, the author takes us through the details of sightlines, from the simplest concept of proscenium theatre to the most elaborate playhouse. He shows how to deal with problems of masking, rigging borders, fixing cycloramas and systems of flying. This is a highly practical book.

SOUTHERN, RICHARD, *Stage Setting* (Faber & Faber).
Starting with the simplest of equipment, the author shows how the scenic theatre can be created. The book is a reminder that even the scenic theatre can start with curtains and screens, and that scenery can be effectively used without having to spend a lot of time and money!

STEWART, HAL D., *Stage Management* (Pitman).
This is a practical handbook for the stage-manager and technician. It deals with scenery and setting, and everything in it is of interest to the designer.

GLOSSARY

Above: Upstage of the point referred to.

Act-drop: A cloth painted to serve for use at the end of an act, instead of using the curtain.

Apron stage: The part of the stage on the auditorium side of the proscenium. A forestage (q.v.) but usually (*a*) portable (often covering an orchestra pit), (*b*) not integrated with proscenium doors and/or boxes, (*c*) sometimes at a different (lower) level from the main stage.

Architectural setting: A permanent background to the acting area, usually in a theatre with an open stage (q.v.) and designed integrally with the auditorium.

Architrave: The moulding that surrounds a door or window frame.

Arena: An acting area that is (*a*) on floor level as opposed to raised (a stage), (*b*) partially or wholly surrounded by the audience as an open stage, not an enclosed stage.

Backdrop: A cloth painted to provide a view of the distance.

Backing: Usually a flat set behind a door, window or other aperture to provide a view beyond and to conceal offstage space, etc.

Bar: Short for barrel, a metal tube (usually of 2-in. diameter standard scaffolding) used for carrying lighting equipment and either flown from the grid (q.v.) or mounted vertically as a boom (q.v.).

Batten: A length of wood (*a*) to which a cloth is tacked at top and bottom, (*b*) to which lamp-holders are screwed to form a row of lights and hence, (*c*) batten-holder, a lamp-socket for screwing to woodwork, etc.

Below: Downstage of the point referred to.

Book-flat: Two flats hinged together and able to stand independently.

Boom: (*a*) A vertical lighting bar (q.v.) usually in the wings, (*b*) a wheeled truck with several levels for painting scenery (American).

Booth stage: A raised platform, part of which is curtained off to form a tiring house (q.v.) and the remainder forming an acting area open to the audience on three sides. *See* sketch on page 9.

Borders: Curtains or flats suspended so as to mask in over the acting area.

Box set: Scenery made up of flats arranged to represent the walls (and ceiling) of a room.

Brace: A support for a flat usually made from a wooden strut (or two pieces that extend) fitted with a special hook, for engaging in a screw-eye, and a base plate to take a stage screw or weight.

Canvas: Material made of cotton (for making flats and cloths).

Carpet-cut: A narrow trap running across the stage, at the setting line, with a hinged flap that will trap and hold the downstage edge of a floor cloth.

Cleat: A wooden or hardware projection (sometimes simply a screw) giving a hold for lashline (q.v.) on the back of the flat.

Cloth: Canvas made up by sewing widths together for painting backdrops, floor coverings, etc.

Composite set: Scenery representing simultaneously several different places all of which are on stage.

Counterweight: A special weight used to balance scenery, etc. that is suspended from the grid (q.v.) and enabling it to be flown in and out easily.

Curtain: The main curtains that close the proscenium arch.

Cutcloth: A cloth with the middle cut out to provide side and overhead pieces (instead of wings and a border) and usually with an uneven profile, painted to represent such things as trees, rocks, clouds, etc.

Cyclorama: A curved wall, or heavy canvas cloth, with an even surface, at the back of a stage and lit to simulate the sky.

Dimmer: A piece of electrical apparatus (there are many sorts) that gives control over the brightness of lighting.

Dip: A pocket in the stage floor covered by a flap allowing flexible cable to be plugged into an electric socket.

Downstage: Towards the audience.

Downstage left, right, centre: See diagram on page 27.

Drop-curtain: A curtain that is flown rather than parted in the middle.

Drugget: Matting or canvas usually put down in the wings to reduce the noise of feet offstage.

Enclosed stage: A stage separated from the auditorium by a wall (the stage wall), and having an acting area viewed from the audience through the proscenium (q.v.).

End stage: An open stage (q.v.) set across one end of the room.

False proscenium: A large arch, usually made of flats, set upstage of the inner proscenium (q.v.). It is usually designed as a scenic unit, but it may serve merely to reduce the proscenium opening.

Fitch: A small paint brush. A lining fitch has its hairs cut diagonally to facilitate painting straight lines.

Flat: A piece of scenery made of canvas stretched on a wooden frame.

Flies: The space over the stage and above sightlines into which suspended scenery, etc. can be hoisted by lines from the grid when it is struck for storage.

Float: A wagon or other vehicle decorated, often with scenic units.

Floats: Footlights. The term belongs to the time when light came from wicks floating in oil.

Flood: A lantern, usually with a reflector, that throws a wide beam of light.

Fly-rail: A rail to which is fixed a series of cleats for tying off the ropes carrying, over the grid, scenery, etc.

Footlights: A row of lights across the stage in front of the tabs (q.v.) and sometimes let into a trough (q.v.).

Forestage: Part of the stage in front of the setting line and, in old theatres, enclosed by the proscenium with its doors and boxes.

French brace: A wooden triangular support hinged to the back of a flat (usually a low flat or groundrow).

Front-of-house: In the auditorium and not on-stage. Particularly front-of-house spotlights.

Get-out: The removal of scenery, etc. from a theatre.

Grid: A series of beams (usually R.S.J.s), over the stage, running parallel to the stage wall, equipped with pulleys and ropes so that scenery, lighting, etc. can be suspended, and usually high enough to allow cloths to be flown out of sight from the audience for scene changes.

Groundrow: A low flat, running across the stage, and often with an uneven profile, painted to represent middle distance.

Inner proscenium: Made of tormentors, teaser and returns (q.v.) masks the space between proscenium and setting, and provides for a prompt corner, perch spots, and (sometimes) entrances; it is usually fixed, more or less permanently, and is often made of black velvet or other unobtrusive material.

Iron: The safety curtain, in big theatres usually made of steel, and running in vertical channels fixed to the stage wall. It is an important element in safety precautions, sealing off the enclosed stage from the auditorium.

Jog: (a) A narrow flat, (b) to set flats at a right-angle to each other.

Lashline: A piece of rope (usually sash cord) fixed to the top corner of a flat and providing a means to lace it to a neighbouring flat, using cleats (q.v.).

Leg: A width of curtain serving as a wing or flat.

Lines: (a) The words learned by an actor, (b) the ropes used with the grid system for suspending scenery, etc.

Masking: Concealing from view; interrupting sightlines (q.v.).

O.P.: Opposite prompt, or stage right. *See* Prompt.

Open stage: A stage that is in the same space as the auditorium, i.e. not an enclosed stage (q.v.). *See also* End stage, Theatre in the round, Transverse stage, Three-sided stage.

Orchestra: A pit in front of the stage (and often extending under it) to house musicians. In origin (with the Greek theatre) the circular arena used as acting area.

Pageant: (a) A type of entertainment usually epic, episodic and historical, (b) a decorated cart or float, (c) a floodlight of a special sort, with reflector and spill rings, giving a strong beam of light.

Paint: A mixture of powdered colouring matter, size, and water for painting scenery. Also, of course, other colouring media.

Paint frame: A large frame, able to carry a set of flats or a full-sized cloth, suspended (usually close to a wall) and counterweighted so that it can sink through the floor thus enabling a painter to work on scenery from floor level.

Perch: The positions on the stage wall of spotlights providing side lighting. Originally the platforms from which limelights were operated.

Periaktoi: Vertical prism-shaped scenic units that (according to Vitruvius) could be revolved to present three different pictures to the audience in classical Greek theatre.

Permanent set: Scenery that stands throughout the play.

Prompt: (a) A reminder given to the actor who has forgotten his words, hence (b) the place, or side of the stage (usually the left side, facing the audience), where the prompter stands.

Proscenium: (*a*) The space in the stage wall through which the audience sees the acting area, (*b*) the stage wall itself, (*c*) the stage itself (but this is not modern usage) or that part of the stage between the curtain and the orchestra containing the proscenium arch.

Proscenium line: An imaginary line drawn across the stage from one side of the proscenium opening to the other, and on the upstage side of the proscenium opening.

Rail: Horizontal member of a flat.

Rake: (*a*) The slope on the stage floor for helping perspective effects, (*b*) the slope on the auditorium floor for helping sightlines (q.v.).

Render: Give a finish to paintwork by providing texture, shadows, etc.

Return: A flat or curtain set at a right-angle to another; particularly the flat at a right-angle to the tormentor (q.v.).

Reveal: (*a*) The thickness of a flat, (*b*) the part of a door frame that suggests the thickness of a wall.

Revolve: A circular truck with a central axis for scene changing, etc.

Rostrum: An independent platform for scenic use, and usually portable.

Scene dock: Storage room where scenery is stacked.

Scenery: Flats, cloths and other units that are painted and put on stage to form a background or locale for the acting area, and usually for a particular "scene" or part of a play.

Set: (*a*) Put scenery, etc. in its correct position for the performance, (*b*) short for setting (q.v.) as in Box set, etc.

Setting: Scenery, curtains, cyclorama, portable units and permanent units that can be used on the acting area as a background or locale for any play.

Setting line: An imaginary line drawn across the stage, usually immediately upstage of the inner proscenium (q.v.), marking the downstage limit for setting scenery.

Sightlines: (*a*) The uninterrupted view of the stage by members of the audience, hence (*b*) the lines marking the limits of such uninterrupted viewing, and (*c*) any possible view from seating in the auditorium to the stage.

Size: A glue that is mixed with colour and water to make scene-paint and prevents the paint from powdering off the scenery.

Skeleton set: Scenery that suggests locale by using outline frames, or cut-down flats, usually in front of a cyclorama or in a curtained surround.

Skip: A hamper for carrying costumes.

Sky-cloth: A large cloth hung at the back of the stage to represent the sky, instead of a cyclorama (q.v.).

Sloat: A trap (*a*) with guides for taking a lift, (*b*) running across the stage and designed to take cloths; one can be dropped straight in from its flown position (the canvas folding in zigzags), its lines unhooked and attached to the cloth required for the next scene.

Splatter: Throw drops of paint on the canvas to give texture, etc.

Spot: Short for spotlight, a lantern with an optical system (of reflector, lenses and a special lamp) providing a controlled beam of light.

Stage cloth: A heavy canvas cloth that covers the floor of the acting area. It is usually painted as an integral part of the setting.

Stile: Vertical member of framework for a flat.

Stipple: Push paint on to the canvas, with a fairly dry brush, to give texture, etc.

Strike: Remove scenery, etc. from its set position.

Tabs: Short for tableau, curtains that part in the middle and close to fill in the proscenium.

Teaser: A border that is usually part of the inner proscenium (q.v.).

Theatre in the round: A theatre with an acting area (usually an arena but sometimes raised) that is surrounded by the auditorium, giving a form of open stage (q.v.).

Three-sided stage: An open stage (q.v.) against one wall of the room which may provide an architectural background, and having the other three sides open to the audience.

Throwline: Lashline (q.v.).

Tiring house: The old term for the enclosed space at the back of a stage, particularly a booth stage (q.v.), that provided a background and a dressing room.

Tormentor: A curtain or wing (q.v.) that forms part of the inner proscenium, running parallel to the proscenium line.

Transverse stage: An open stage (q.v.) in the middle of a room (usually long and narrow) from wall to wall, dividing the auditorium into two parts.

Trap: A portion of the stage floor that can be lifted to allow for (*a*) entrances from below, (*b*) storage of scenery under the stage.

Traverse: Curtains that part, running across the stage and dividing the acting area so that either the downstage section only or the full stage can be used.

Trough: A trapped space across the stage for taking lighting apparatus that is used (*a*) on the cyclorama or sky-cloth, etc. (*b*) for footlights.

Truck: A platform (usually low) on wheels that can take part of or the whole setting including usually acting area space, and used for changing scenery.

Upstage: Away from the audience.

Upstage left, right, centre: See diagram on page 27.

Wings: Flats set at each side of the acting area and more or less parallel to the proscenium line.

INDEX

(Roman numerals refer to plates)